Life Runners

Daily Devotions

Edited by:

DR. PATRICK CASTLE

BERNADETTE COSTELLO

En Route Books and Media, LLC

St. Louis, MO

En Route Books and Media, LLC
5705 Rhodes Avenue
St. Louis, MO 63109

Cover artwork:
"Mother of Life" by Nellie Edwards
Cover design by Kelli Dorrell

LCCN: 2020952330
ISBN-13: 978-1-952464-42-3
Copyright © 2021 LIFE Runners

All rights reserved. No part of this book may be reproduced, stored in a retrieval system, or transmitted in any form, or by any means, without the prior written permission of LIFE Runners. Recitation is permitted.

Introduction

All In Christ for Pro-Life! The LIFE Runners apostolate began by sharing these prayer-filled, challenging, one-minute devotions to help end abortion through holy teamwork. May this daily devotional inspire you to put your Pro-Life faith into action!

Following an encounter with Saint Padre Pio near the finish of the 2006 Pikes Peak mountain race, Dr. Patrick Castle was inspired to lead an *Unbound* book study about how evil works in the modern world. The original group of twelve faithful LIFE Runners identified abortion as the crown jewel of satan. They put their Pro-Life faith into action by writing these devotions, praying for mothers at abortion facilities, and visiting the elderly at nursing homes.

Now, thousands of LIFE Runners, newborns to elderly, in thousands of cities around the world, defend life from conception to eternity. Running is optional, and faith is required. LIFE Runners wear the **REMEMBER The Unborn** message as a public witness on shirts, jackets, hats, wristbands, and more. Their bold blue witness gear impacts hearts and minds for saving lives. LIFE Runners gather for an annual fall race retreat, the summer A-Cross America Relay, and many local chapter huddles. Join the team and order your witness gear at liferunners.org.

Thanks be to God for growing the LIFE Runners apostolate to help end abortion soonest. Special thanks to the 108 authors (index pg 367) for sharing these devotions, En Route for publishing, plus Larry and Diane Cochran for sponsoring this holy project. Thanks to all LIFE Runners who are living out Christ's call to share the gospel of life abundantly. Heaven is a team effort; forward in faith we go.

Therefore, since we are surrounded by such a great cloud of witnesses, let us persevere in running this race set before us with our eyes fixed on Jesus. ~ Heb 12:1-2

GOD first, LIFE always, TEAM forever!

Pray the LIFE Runners Creed to end abortion today:

We believe in the dignity of all human life from conception to natural death.

We run as a **Prayer**, to defend children in the womb, so that they may be born and united with our Christian community.

We run to build **Endurance**, for the race is long and we must keep our eyes fixed on You Lord.

We run for **Awareness**, so our culture will view all human life as a reflection of Your glory Lord.

We run for **Charity**, to provide support for mothers and fathers tempted to abort their child, and healing support for post-abortion women, men, and families.

We run to **End abortion**, for Christ died so that all may live. Guard us all, born and unborn, with Your **PEACE**, Lord. For in You, life is victorious.

We pray and run in Your name, **JESUS CHRIST**. Amen.

Our Lady of Guadalupe, pray for us. **Saint Padre Pio**, pray for us. **Saint Michael the Archangel**, defend us in battle…

Excerpts from Devotions

"When magnified, our first cell at conception, looks like a communion host, the Body of Christ. The cell's surrounding corona radiata is like a monstrance."
~ Dr. Patrick Castle (Jan 23)

"If we do not crucify our flesh with its passions and desires, our carnal desires will crucify our minds."
~ Dr. Rich Reich (Jul 28)

"When we are daunted by the size of the task and keenly aware of our limitations, we are called to take risks with the tools that God has given us." ~ Jeanne Mancini (Jan 10)

"Let us consider then how we may spur one another towards love and life. Let us love, not in word or speech, but in truth and action." ~ Paul Westendorf (Mar 6)

"We must intensify our prayers and fasting for a new birth of freedom so that life and liberty is granted for all, born and unborn." ~ Bishop Robert Gruss (Mar 28)

"Unity"
by Steve Castle

Jan 1

They do not belong to the world any more than I belong to the world. ~ Jn 17:16

We are aliens in a foreign land. Our life is not our own. We were bought at a price; the blood of the cross. We love because Christ first loved us. As Christians we stand on these truths. Jesus reminds us of our inheritance in His high priestly prayer to the Father. We don't belong to the world. Because of this the world will always hate us. This spiritual battle is waged every day in the hearts and minds of those perpetuating the lies of the abortion industry. Let us together pray for unity, All In Christ for Pro-Life!

Today's Challenge: Let us stand firm in our commitment to pray for our enemies and those who harm the least of these through the abortion industry.

"Love Those Who Condemn"

Jan 2

by Scott Casmer

Believe in the Lord Jesus and you and your household will be saved. ~ Act 16:31

Paul and Silas were cited for "disturbing our city" and "advocating customs that are not lawful for us Romans to adopt or practice." Paul had invoked the name of Jesus to exorcise a spirit from a slave who was being unjustly used by her owners for profit. The public condemned them and had them jailed. Upon being freed, Paul and Silas did not seek revenge on the jailer, but instead shared their faith and baptized his whole family. This passage has analogies to those engaged in the Pro-Life movement who are condemned for showing Jesus' love for all human life. Our Pro-Life message is not welcomed by those who work to uphold the misguided laws that allow for the destruction of human life. Thankfully, the Holy Spirit strengthens us to love those who condemn us.

Today's Challenge: Identify those in your life who would benefit from understanding the sanctity of life. Pray for their conversion and for an opportunity to discuss life issues.

"Silent Scream"

by Alton Pelowski

Jan 3

Like a sheep He was led to the slaughter, and as a lamb before its shearer is silent, so He opened not His mouth. ~ Act 8:32

Jesus Christ, who suffered in silence for our sake, radically united Himself to the lost and abandoned, and ultimately conquered the power of sin and death. Nowhere is such silent abandonment more present in our world today than in abortion. Following his conversion, the late Bernard Nathanson produced the Pro-Life documentary, "The Silent Scream". The co-founder of NARAL and once a notorious abortionist, Nathanson grew to realize the humanity of the unborn and later, because of the witness of others, came to faith in Christ. So, too, will many people blinded by the culture of death come to know the reality of abortion and Christ's saving power if believers obey the prompting of the Spirit and are willing to humbly witness to the truth.

Today's Challenge: The next time someone makes a comment about your Pro-Life faith, don't be afraid to engage.

Jan 4 — "More Than Loose Change"

By Pastor Steve

Then Peter took him by the right hand and raised him up, and immediately his feet and ankles grew strong.
~ Act 3:7

Many of us focus on finances when Christ is wanting us to have so much more. This man trusted in Peter's faith, and then he ran! This man was crippled from birth - can you imagine the shock, amazement and joy that he had. He thought he was getting loose change and he received so much more. Is there something in your life where you have felt crippled for a long time? Reach to Christ. He will lift you up and do you see what happens? You will leap for joy. Others will be filled with amazement and worship the one true God.

Today's Challenge: Are you merely looking for loose change when Jesus is telling you to rise up and walk? What do you need to take Christ's hand and get up and walk? You can do it.

"Our Comfort Zone"
by Paul Westendorf

Jan 5

Jesus was standing on the shore; but the disciples did not realize that it was Jesus. ~ Jn 21:4

It is easy to become uncertain of your faith and give in to despair. There are constant attacks on religious freedoms and organizations, the family and marriage, on unborn lives, on the sick and elderly with assisted suicide. We hear the rhetoric over and over and it can make us wonder, "Should I speak out for justice? What will others think if I live out the Pro-Life message?" Jesus calls all of us out of our comfort zone to share His message of love and forgiveness, to speak the Truth.

Today's Challenge: What are you doing? Fix your eyes on the Lord, get outside your comfort zone, and remain steadfast in your commitment to see Jesus in the unborn "least of these."

Jan 6 — "Sign of the Cross"
by Dr. Rich Reich

Now this was the second sign Jesus did when He came to Galilee from Judea. ~ Jn 4:54

John records the second sign that Jesus did in which He performed a remote healing of a royal official's son. Jesus recognized that "unless people see signs and wonders, they do not believe". Despite the many signs that Jesus performed in the people's presence, they refused to believe in Him. So, Jesus gave everyone a final sign: the Sign of the Cross, by dying for us to atone for our sins. Today we are surrounded by miracles, but our world does not recognize them. Our culture needs to recognize that every child, born and unborn, is a miracle.

Today's Challenge: We must also take an active role in protecting God's creation. Help others to see the miracle in the creation of every human life.

"Poverty of Spirit"
by Greg Robeson

Jan 7

Whoever receives one child such as this in My name, receives Me; and whoever receives Me, receives not Me but the One who sent Me. ~ Mk 9:37

There are many aspects of being childlike that Jesus emphasizes, such as innocence, trust, simplicity, and dependence on another. But here, being like a child means being "poor in spirit." Our culture loathes poverty as something to be avoided like a disease, however it offers our souls potential enrichment. Being poor in spirit is a disposition, an attitude that takes every instance of doing without, and turns it into a celebration of the way Christ lives more fully in us. Paul embodies this when he says, "I live no longer but Christ lives in me."

Today's Challenge: Let's pray for each other, that our will would be united in suffering for the unborn, the greatest class of innocents being persecuted today. It is only when Christ dwells in us that we are ready for supernatural battle, the type of battle being fought today for the unborn.

Jan 8 — "Billboards for Life"
by Dr. Rich Reich

He sighed from the depth of His spirit and said, 'Why does this generation seek a sign?' ~ Mk 8:12

People are walking billboards as they take pride showing off their brand name clothes. Companies understand the power of brands very well. Consumers have become so obsessed about brands that they are more interested in the logo than the product itself. God wants us to believe in His power and love without needing a miracle or sign. However, we can use the infatuation with logos and signs to bring attention to the greatest cause, defending God's gift of Life. 80% of post-abortion mothers said they would have chosen life if just one person had encouraged them as a sign of God's love. We ought to be that encouraging person, a living sign, impacting hearts and minds for saving lives.

Today's Challenge: Wear your LIFE Runners gear in public as a living sign, a personal billboard, helping all to "REMEMBER The Unborn."

"Shine!"
by Dana Cody

Jan 9

In the same way, let your light shine before men, that they may see your good deeds and praise your Father in Heaven. ~ Mt 5:16

Our culture is similar to that of Jerusalem when the city was infiltrated by evil. Nehemiah was able to restore Jerusalem by speaking the truth to its inhabitants and restoring the wall that kept evil out. Nehemiah let his light shine, and the wall was restored. You can rebuild the wall that will protect the unborn from the evil of abortion. Let your light shine and speak the Gospel of life to our culture.

Today's Challenge: Pray the LIFE Runners Creed to help end abortion.

Jan 10

"David vs Goliath"
by Jeanne Mancini

For the battle belongs to the Lord. ~ 1 Sm 17:47

Goliath is much more experienced, has a larger staff, and all the best tools. David is young, inexperienced, probably alone, and brings only a sling and a few stones. By all human calculations, David is going to be clobbered by Goliath. Don't we often feel like David vs. Goliath as we strive to restore a culture of life? Abortion proponents have more money, more lobbyists, the best tools that money can buy. When we are daunted by the size of the task and keenly aware of our limitations, we are called, like David, to take risks with the tools that God has given us. The Creator of the universe will use our humble efforts to bring about something much bigger than what we could have accomplished on our own. In the end, "the battle is the Lord's."

Today's Challenge: Write a Pro-Life opinion editorial for your local newspaper.

"Harder Than It Sounds"
by Fr. Andrew Dickinson

Jan 11

If anyone says, 'I love God,' but hates his brother, he is a liar; for whoever does not love a brother whom he has seen cannot love God whom he has not seen. ~ 1 Jn 4:20

We live in a romantic world that makes love seem light and easy. affection is an invitation to love, it is not love itself. Love is shown in the fullness of living, not just in the affection. To love is to choose the good of another, even when it is difficult. Love when it hurts, love when it isn't easy, love when it is messy. We build a culture of love one trial at a time. To build a culture of life, we must first build a culture of love.

Today's Challenge: Prepare your own heart for great acts of love and create empathy for those who struggle to love the unborn.

Jan 12

"Relish the Wonder"
by Dianne Overmann

In this is love: not that we have loved God, but that He loved us and sent His Son as expiation for our sins.
~ 1 Jn 4:10

We have heard of God's love. We can think of the tremendous love expressed by God when He became human. The blessings God has given us have been so numerous they would fill more than a few baskets with extras. Answered prayers and help and guidance have always been there. Yet, we let ourselves return to the pains, the confusions, and the fears of today and wonder where our loving God is. God is present among us today and every day, explicit in the conception of each child, made in His image.

Today's Challenge: "Rejoice in the Lord always. Again, I say rejoice."

"Peace Be With You"
by Dr. Rich Reich

Jan 13

For the sake of my brothers and friends I say, 'Peace be with you.' ~ Ps 122:8

Jesus often greeted His disciples with the saying, "Peace be with you"; however, Jesus would have spoken to His disciples in Aramaic saying, "schlomo". Schlomo is a wish for an abundance of blessings. In Jesus' case, it is not merely a wish, because He has the power to do what He says. Jesus does not wish peace, He gives it. The peace that Jesus gives is the schlomo of God, a supernatural peace of spiritual completeness. His peace is much more profound, healing, strengthening, and lasting than anything the world can offer.

Today's Challenge: When someone is praying in front of an abortion facility, there is an up to 70% appointment no show rate. Peacefully pray in front of an abortion facility to help end abortion in your community.

.

Jan 14 — "Thy Will Be Done"
by Jeff Grabosky

This is how you are to pray: 'Our Father who art in Heaven, hallowed be Thy Name, Thy Kingdom come, Thy will be done, on earth as it is in Heaven. ~ Mt 6:9-10

We have all prayed the Lord's prayer countless times. Slow down and focus on the words that we are praying for God's will to be carried out on Earth. If we are truly involved in the prayer being a conversation with God, then we should always be listening to God in how we can follow His instructions on what we can do to carry out His holy will. Each and every one of us was created by God in love to be a light to this world. We all have a unique set of gifts that is meant to be used in a certain way to glorify God. In using our God-given gifts, we can change this world into a place that values the precious gift of life.

Today's Challenge: Spend time slowly praying the Our Father and listen to God speaking to you. Pray today for the wisdom to learn and the fortitude to carry out the will of the Father.

"Blessed Are They"
by Allan Parker

Jan 15

Blessed are you when they insult you and persecute you and utter every kind of evil against you falsely because of Me. Rejoice and be glad, for your reward will be great in Heaven. ~ Mt 5:11-12

These grace-filled words are especially applicable to the Pro-Life movement. All of us long for the day when Roe vs Wade will be overturned. We hunger and thirst for the day when children in the womb and mothers and fathers are protected by law. We long for the day when evil will no longer be called good, but right thinking and right laws will prevail according to God's word.

Today's Challenge: Pray for the day that abortion will be unthinkable. Do not worry, but seek first His Kingdom.

Jan 16

"Discipleship"
by Dr. Rich Reich

He called His disciples to Himself, and from them He chose twelve, whom He also named apostles. ~ Lk 6:13

Discipleship focuses on actively following in the footsteps of Jesus by putting our faith into action. As disciples of Christ, we share in His mission, His Joy, and His sufferings. Do not waiver in your commitment to protect the dignity of all human life. Be patient with those who do not share in our beliefs. Pray for them and be an example of God's love. There will be sacrifice and discrimination for our beliefs. Nothing is more important than following Jesus and no mission is more important than protecting the dignity of all human life.

Today's Challenge: Be an authentic disciple of Christ and a servant of the unborn.

"If God is for us"
by Stephanie Kemp

Jan 17

If God is for us, who can be against us? ~ Rom 8:31

The Master of the universe and the Author of life holds all things in His Hands. We just have to be His pencil as St. Mother Teresa advised. Look at what God has given us! He spared nothing. He has given us everything, including the gift of Himself. Are we willing to devote our time, talent and treasure to the cause of protecting all human life? In Jesus, we find the courage and perseverance to meet each new day despite our fears and our setbacks; and we find the compassion to reach out to those who are in need and those who are hurting from abortion.

Today's Challenge: Reflect on the role you play in continuing the mission of Jesus. Are you willing to enter God's will and trust that the smallest thing you do makes a difference?

Jan 18

"Dark to Light"
by Molly McDonald

Do you not know that if you present yourselves to someone as obedient slaves, you are slaves of the one you obey, either of sin, which leads to death, or of obedience, which leads to righteousness? ~ Rom 6:16

How can abortion facility workers happily usher in a mother to kill their innocent unborn child? It is so easy to look onto the abortion facility workers with an attitude of "they should know better," but in reality they can't know better until they are open to the truth from our Lord Jesus Christ. They have all become victims and slaves to the lies of the devil. We need to continue praying for them. There is hope, and we are reminded of this hope when we hear the great news of another abortion facility worker quitting or a facility closing. Let's go meet those who are in the dark and invite them to the light of life!

Today's Challenge: Say a prayer for all those in the dark, especially those who support abortion, that they may have a change of heart, and turn to the light of God.

"Vulnerable"
by Kathy Forck

Jan 19

Present yourselves to God as raised from the dead to life and the parts of your bodies to God as weapons for righteousness. ~ Rom 6:13

This is so true for those witnessing against abortion who use their bodies "as weapons for righteousness" and thus make themselves vulnerable to abortion facility workers and bystanders. It is easy for us to think it is hopeless to stop the murder of babies. It is easy to be overwhelmed by the sheer numbers lost each day, but our God has given us the grace to do "something". We see God's miracles as we witness for babies, mothers and families. God has given us so much, and we must give so much more to this cause for life.

Today's Challenge: Prayer presence in front of abortion facilities is working, it is saving babies and mothers. If you are able, please take a prayerful stand.

Jan 20 — "Redemptive"
by Jeff Grabosky

With the Lord there is mercy, and fullness of redemption.
~ Ps 130:7

We all have sinned and are therefore in need of redemption. God not only forgives our sins, but He also grants us graces. Half of abortions are repeat abortions. For a post-abortion mother who is redeemed, she will have the grace to choose life for her next child. God can truly turn any situation into a blessing. It is up to us, however, to repent of our sins and to trust in his goodness and mercy. God is waiting for us to return to Him. We can take confidence in His mercy and should be quick to share this good news for post-abortion healing.

Today's Challenge: Pray the Divine Mercy chaplet for healing abortion wounds. Lord, have mercy on us and the whole world.

"Harden Not Your Hearts"
by Tonchi Weaver

Jan 21

Oh that today you would hear His voice, do not harden your hearts. ~ Ps 95:7-8

God's Law is written on our hearts, and the seeds of truth take root. The miraculous blending of male and female at the point of conception is pure creation. The child formed at the moment of conception is as complete as the child at nine seconds, nine months, nine years or ninety-nine years. We don't buy into the popular slogans designed to make people comfortable with the new cultural norm, such as "you can't legislate morality" or "if you don't approve of abortion, don't have one" - such thinking hardens hearts.

Today's Challenge: Let God soften your heart with His words, so you can help soften the hearts of others to receive His seeds of truth.

Jan 22

"Compassion"
by Sara Beaner

She stood at His feet weeping and began to bathe His feet with her tears. The Pharisee said, 'If this man were a prophet, He would know who and what sort of woman this is, that she is a sinner.' ~ Lk 7:38-39

Do we know this woman coming to Jesus? Could she be a coworker, sister, friend, neighbor, or complete stranger who had an abortion and is begging Jesus for forgiveness? Do we say to ourselves out of pride, "She is one of those women," and not show compassion or help her? We must treat the broken-hearted women who have had abortions with the same forgiveness that Jesus gives us.

Today's Challenge: The word compassion means "to suffer with." Show compassion for post-abortion women.

"First Baby Photo"
by Dr. Patrick Castle

Jan 23

O Lord God, what good will Your gifts be, if I keep on being childless. ~ Gen 15:2

When magnified, you can see that the zygote, our first cell at conception, looks like a communion host, the Eucharist, the Body of Christ. The cell's surrounding corona radiata is like a monstrance, the holding vessel for the Eucharist. The Eucharist doesn't look like Jesus, and the zygote doesn't look like a person. However, the Eucharist is completely Jesus, and your zygote is completely you!

Today's Challenge: If you can't see your neighbor in the zygote, just wait a few weeks for magnification. If you can't see Jesus in the Eucharist, read Jn 6:35-69 for magnification.

Jan 24 — "Miracles"
by Dr. Rich Reich

'Amen, I say to you, no prophet is accepted in his own native place.' ~ Lk 4:24

We are always searching for the incredible, for something outside of ourselves. The Galileans were blind to see that one of their own could be capable of producing miracles. We can become blind to miracles, because we become ungrateful. We may consider our fortune in life as a bit of luck or something of our own doing. We get so accustomed to God's goodness that it becomes a routine, and then we become blind to the miracles around us. We need to remember that every life is a miracle from God.

Today's Challenge: Wear your LIFE Runners "REMEMBER The Unborn" jersey in public today. This simple courageous act of faith and love could result in the miracle of a life saved.

"People in our Lives"
by Kevin McNicholas

Jan 25

Do not ask me to abandon or forsake you! For wherever you go, I will go, wherever you lodge I will lodge, your people shall be my people, and your God my God.
~ Ru 1:16

Ruth realized that through her faith she would be saved, which is why she stayed with Naomi. God places people in our lives that we need to follow. We pray for "those who have gone before us marked with the sign of faith." These are our priests, pastors, parents, grandparents, relatives, friends, and those whose devout examples bring us closer to God and inspire us to serve "the least of these."

Today's Challenge: Identify a person in your life whose faith in God is an example and inspiration to you. Let them know in person or through prayer, which will encourage their important witness.

"That We May Not Offend"
Jan 26
by Dr. Rich Reich

Take the first fish that comes up. Open its mouth, and you will find a coin worth twice the temple tax. Give that to them for me and for you. ~ Mt 17:27

Jesus paid the temple tax, which He did not owe, so that even the hated tax collectors would have the opportunity to accept Him as their savior. Our mindset should be about advancing God's Kingdom rather than exercising our rights. God is concerned about justice, but it is often through the sufferings from injustice that people see His grace in action. Remember, Jesus allowed Himself to be crucified to pay the tax for our sins.

Today's Challenge: When discussing abortion with those who oppose our Pro-Life view, subdue your passion for the unborn and allow yourself to listen and be heard through peaceful discussions, planting seeds for future conversion.

"Losing One's Life"
by Jenn Garza

Jan 27

For whoever wishes to save his life will lose it, but whoever loses his life for My sake will find it. ~ Mt 16:25

We are all called to lay down our entire lives for the salvation of souls and the glory of God. We are called to lose our lives for those who are so blindly opposed to our cause for life. We thank God for the gift of life by giving our life back to Him and others. Losing one's life for the sake of another is not an easy task. Let us rejoice when the road looks bleak – for Christ surely did not skip through a flowery meadow toward the cross. And after the sacrifices of this life, oh how sweet it will be to enter abundant life in the Kingdom of God.

Today's Challenge: Make a small sacrifice of time in prayer for someone for whom you have never before prayed.

Jan 28 — "Be like the Apostles"
by Shane Kapler

A prophet is not without honor except in his native place and in his own house. ~ Mt. 13:57

In Baptism we began a life of supernatural participation in the life of Jesus - and with it, His role of prophet. Sometimes we fare well when speaking out for the unborn, and at other times not so well. We must not be shocked by the negative encounters; it has always been the lot of the prophet, the lot of Christ's disciples.

Today's Challenge: Wear your LIFE Runners "REMEMBER The Unborn" jersey as a public witness. If you face opposition, imitate the apostles by letting your first words be joyful thanksgiving that you have the honor of participating in Jesus' mission.

"Worker or Disciple"
by Dr. Rich Reich

Jan 29

She had a sister named Mary who sat beside the Lord at His feet listening to Him speak. ~ Lk 10:39

Sometimes we find ourselves so focused on the task at hand that we don't take time to relate to others. Martha complained to the Lord that Mary is not helping her, and Jesus corrects her stating that her sister had chosen the better part. Mary has chosen to be a disciple of Jesus by sitting at His feet and not merely a worker like Martha. The difference between being a worker and a disciple of Christ can be a matter of perspective and attitude. We can become burdened by the details of our Pro-Life work if we do not place God first.

Today's Challenge: Choose the better part, be a disciple rather than merely a worker of the Lord.

Jan 30

"Give Life"
by Amy Kosta

The Son of Man did not come to be served but to serve and to give His life as a ransom for many. ~ Mt 20:28

Rulers of earthly kingdoms make their authority felt in many ways. In our day, rulers have used their authority to ensure that human lives may be lawfully crushed even before they are born. Christ's Kingdom, however, is unlike the kingdoms of earth. Christ would drink the painful "chalice" of His suffering on the cross to defeat sin and death, making everlasting life possible for us.

Today's Challenge: Are we willing to give at least some small part of our lives in the service of unborn life? If so, we can attain that greatness of our King who ransomed His life for us.

"Serpents and Doves"
by Angi Castle

Jan 31

Behold, I am sending you like sheep in the midst of wolves; so be shrewd as serpents and simple as doves. ~ Mt 10:16

Our Christian values regarding the sanctity of life, marriage, and families are under attack by the government that should be pledged to defend them. We don't have to look far to see throngs of people looking the other way as our moral values are destroyed and replaced with the values of long-ago pagans. As the world makes the practice of our faith increasingly difficult, we are called to be increasingly shrewd and simultaneously simple. In order to seek and advance eternal truths, we need to use the cleverness of our minds and the fundamentals of our faith.

Today's Challenge: Be shrewdly simple today. Think about how you can shape your environment to convey the simple message that all life is a gift from God.

| Feb 1 |

"In service of the Gospel"
by Fr. Michael Orsi

The more you sow, the more you reap. ~ 2 Cor 9:6

Putting oneself in the service of the Gospel is the charge that Christ gives all the baptized. Because every human being is made in the image and likeness of God, Jesus is clear of our obligation toward the poor. This is especially true for preservation of the life of unborn babies. Saint Paul reminds us that we will reap what we sow. Our efforts and success in saving the life of the innocent may never be known to us or them in this life, but when all is revealed at the end of time our good deeds will be remembered. Let us run the race and win the prize of eternal life!

Today's Challenge: Put yourself in the service of the Gospel by doing something tangible to protect the innocent, poor, and unborn.

"Ravenous Wolves"
by TD Dorrell

Feb 2

Beware of false prophets who come to you in sheep's clothing, but underneath are ravenous wolves. ~ Mt 7:15

Women in crisis pregnancy situations are lured by the "false prophets" who come to them in sheep's clothing. Almost half of the abortions in America are chosen by young women of college age. These women are often frightened and feel there is no alternative for them but to abort their baby. The false prophets, such as Planned Parenthood, offer the false promise of an easy way of ending their pregnancy when in fact, women are left feeling empty and guilty with emotional scars that last a lifetime. Together we can work toward promoting the culture of life by protecting women from the ravenous wolves and helping them choose life for their babies.

Today's Challenge: Support your local pregnancy help center and let others know about their life saving services.

Feb 3

"Armor or God"
by Pavel Arestov

Therefore take up the whole armor of God, that you may be able to stand firm. ~ Eph 6:13

We live in a world that is drowning in sin and the hearts of many are ruled by darkness. Every day, thousands of lives are ended by abortionists. These abortionists threw down the armor of God and were enslaved by the master of deception and darkness. By putting on the armor of God and wielding the sword of the Spirit, we acquire necessary protection against the wickedness and snares of the devil. God's armor is acquired through prayer, study of God's word and devotion to ministry. We must outcast ourselves from the ways of the world to be God's warriors.

Today's Challenge: Devote yourself to the teachings of Christ, so you can grow in faith and be vigilant of the devil's schemes.

"Be Happy"
by Dr. Rich Reich

Feb 4

He began to teach them. ~ Mt 5:2

Each of the Beatitudes begins with "blessed," which can be interpreted to mean "happy". Jesus teaches that we will be happy by being meek, sorrowful, merciful, and persecuted. The media lures us into materialism for happiness rather than following the Beatitudes. Which guidance brings true happiness? God has written the answer on your heart. If you are persecuted for defending the unborn, have faith and persevere, because Jesus has promised you eternal happiness.

Today's Challenge: Believe in what Jesus teaches on how to be happy and follow the Beatitudes.

| Feb 5 |

"Giving God Your All"
by Dr. Rich Reich

A man ran up, knelt down before Him, and asked Him, 'Good Teacher, what must I do to inherit eternal life?'
~ **Mk 10:17**

The majority of America is against abortion. So why then is abortion legal? It may be that those who support abortion are more active than those who oppose it. So, for those who oppose abortion, what must we do? The rich man asked Jesus what he must do. Jesus replied that he must give everything. As Christians, we are called to give everything; 99% will not do. Jesus gave us everything when He died on the cross. We should give everything of ourselves in return.

Today's Challenge: Defend the unborn with all your heart, with all your soul, with all your strength, and with all your mind. Lives are counting on us.

"Love and Fidelity"
by Shane Kapler

Feb 6

They are no longer two but one flesh. Therefore what God has joined together, no human being must separate.
~ Mk 10:8-9

In a very real sense, the culture of death has only been able to arise because the culture of love – of marital love – has been in a state of decay. Our culture's understanding of marriage has been cheapened, along with the sacrificial nature of sexuality and parenthood. Where the life-long faithfulness of husband and wife is not prized, the sexual act loses its whole reason for being. As a result, pre-marital sex flourishes, unplanned pregnancies occur – and the environment becomes ripe for abortion.

Today's Challenge: To thoroughly understand Jesus' teaching about marriage, read Paragraph 1601 of the *Catechism of the Catholic Church* and be inspired!

Feb 7

"Love God's Law"
by Alton Pelowski

Those who love Your law have great peace, and for them there is no stumbling block. ~ Ps 119:165

The law of God does not restrict freedom but rather teaches us how to be truly free. Our freedom is directly related to the truth of how we are created. By contrast, the culture of death doesn't recognize God's law and reduces freedom to simply the choice between options. This inevitably results in a conflict of the strong against the weak and voiceless. Far from bringing great peace, denying God's law leads only to despair and heartache. Building a culture of life begins with the joyful and peaceful witness of those who love God's law.

Today's Challenge: Do you believe that loving God's law will bring great peace? Can others see this peace manifested in your life?

"Consecrated in Truth"
by Alice Chapman

Feb 8

As you have sent Me into the world, so I sent them into the world. And I consecrate Myself for them, so that they also may be consecrated in truth. ~ Jn 17:18-19

Despite the obstacles we face in our spiritual and physical journey on earth, Jesus reminds us that we are never left alone. We are sent into the world consecrated in truth through Jesus' death and resurrection. This gives us courage to speak out and witness for the sanctity of human life even in a hostile political and social climate. Truth prevails.

Today's Challenge: Remember that you are consecrated in truth. Share the gospel of life with someone you meet today.

Feb 9

"Ask In Faith"
by Lauren Muzyka

'What do you want me to do for you?' The blind man replied, 'Master, I want to see.' ~ Mk 10:51

We have to ask for help! We have to be willing to humble ourselves, get on our knees, go to the Lord in prayer, and ask Him for what we need. Quite often, He is simply waiting for us to ask in faith; and as He makes Himself available to us, we must respond in return. God is big enough to take even the holocaust of abortion and end it. But we must be willing to pray, to trust, and then act in faith.

Today's Challenge: Get on your knees today and entrust your biggest prayer requests to Our Lord, knowing He will answer you. Ask God how you can help end abortion.

"Uncomplicated"

by Jason Peters

Feb 10

"Go into the whole world and proclaim the gospel to every creature." ~ Mk 16:15

We are able to show others Jesus in the simplest of ways. Jesus tells us that the Kingdom of Heaven belongs to children. They allow themselves to be open to God. They don't complicate it. We need to simplify our relationship with Christ. Like an unborn child in the womb that relies totally on his or her mother, we need to depend on God. This allows us to be a reflection of Jesus to all those around us.

Today's Challenge: Simplify your relationship with God and proclaim the gospel of life to everyone you know.

| Feb 11 |

"JOY!"

by Amy Kosta

Shout joyfully to God, all the earth, sing praise to the glory of His name; proclaim His glorious praise. ~ **Ps 66:2**

We have many reasons to be joyful! Our Lord and Savior died for our sins, and then He rose again to give us new life. We should celebrate His gift of new life by dedicating ourselves earnestly to the Pro-Life cause. We can do great things with God at our side. We rejoice each time a child is saved from the tragedy of abortion. We know the race is long, but we will endure and run to the finish line with confidence.

Today's Challenge: The word confidence means "with faith." Offer yourself to God and have confidence that He will do great things through you!

"Above All"
by Jenn Garza

Feb 12

The one who is of the earth is earthly and speaks of earthly things. But the one who comes from Heaven is above all.
~ Jn 3:31

In the times we feel defeated or struck down in our effort to protect the unborn, we must remember that the day of our victory is safe in the hands of our Creator. When every so often, we seem to lose a battle here on earth, let us remain hopeful in the knowledge that we are winning the heavenly war. If the one who comes from Heaven is above all, then all we do must be done for Him. The moments when the mountains seem too high to reach, remember He is above all.

Today's Challenge: This week offer up a mile for someone. Pray that people will begin to see Christ in you more clearly!

Feb 13

"The Light"
by Molly McDonald

Whoever lives the truth comes to the light, so that his works may be clearly seen as done in God. ~ Jn 3:21

We are living in the light of God when we are a public witness, wearing a LIFE Runners jersey, praying at an abortion facility, and posting the truth on social media. We live in a culture of death that leads people to do wicked things and stray from the light. Those who run from the light have bought into the lie of the pro-abortion agenda and are being led into the darkness. It's easier to go with the cultural ways than against. Pray to lead souls away from the darkness and into the light of truth.

Today's Challenge: Pray for those who believe the lie of abortion, that they may have a change of heart, and turn to the light of God.

"Apathy Kills"
by Dr. Patrick Castle

Feb 14

And let us not grow weary of doing good, for in due season we will reap, if we do not give up. ~ Gal 6:9

Apathy has allowed Planned Parenthood to kill millions of babies. Why doesn't the media report this daily massacre? Perhaps our apathetic culture is too selfish to care about the defenseless unborn. Or perhaps many believe that ending abortion is out of their control. That is wrong! We can make a difference. Apathy means an absence of passion. Renew your passion by remembering the passion of Christ and what He did for us. Let His passion fuel your ministry to share the gospel of life so others do not become apathetic.

Today's Challenge: Are we apathetic to the thousands of unborn babies slaughtered every day? Do not let apathy kill. Stay passionate about the unborn.

Feb 15

"Rise Up!"
by Dr. Patrick Castle

Jesus said to him, "Rise up, take your mat, walk... sin no more." ~ Jn 5:8

While we may or may not be suffering from a physical ailment or impairment, sin spiritually impairs our lives. What a great gift that Christ gives us in the Sacrament of Reconciliation, forgiving our sins and bestowing His mercy and love upon us. Christ spiritually heals us and sends us back into the world to be His hands and feet for the unborn, the disabled, the elderly, the infirm. May we be open to God's grace to be transformed by Christ crucified in order to rise up and walk with Him, the author of life.

Today's Challenge: Make a good examination of conscience and go to the Sacrament of Reconciliation.

"My Neighbor"
by Dr. Patrick Castle

Feb 16

Love your neighbor as yourself. ~ Mk 12:31

Planned Parenthood is not a nice neighbor. But as the Gospel states, we are called to love those who work there or visit the facilities. Does that mean we let them continue with their actions? Of course not! If your neighbor was backing out of the driveway and a child ran into his or her blindspot, you should stop them. Wouldn't you want someone to give you the same warning? Caring about your neighbor includes some tough love, but it doesn't mean degrade them or be apathetic in an effort to be tolerant. We must help our neighbors grow to be the best beings God created them to be.

Today's Challenge: Take some time to pray outside an abortion facility. Be there to help them to the side of truth and life.

Feb 17

"Fulfilled"
by Dave DiNuzzo

I have come not to abolish but to fulfill. ~ Mt. 5:17

The Beatitudes are radically counter-cultural, and in them we find freedom and fulfillment. We should be poor in spirit, gentle, hunger for righteousness, merciful, pure in heart, and peacemakers. When persecutions come along, we should rejoice in the fact that the Kingdom of Heaven is ours! These characteristics are the fulfillment of God's law for true freedom. A culture that devalues human life is not embracing Christ's Beatitudes.

Today's Challenge: Commit to daily faith steps so as to grow closer to the Lord. As Christ Himself exemplified, unite any suffering you may be feeling to His suffering on the Cross.

"Deepest Beliefs"
by Shane Kapler

Feb 18

They seek Me day after day, and desire to know My ways, like a nation that has done what is just and not abandoned the law of their God. ~ Is 58:2

Many are blind to the impact of legalized abortion on gradually warping minds and hearts, of gradually eroding the dignity we attach to all life. The loudest cultural voice does not respect the sanctity of marriage, denying that a mother and father are integral for the healthy development of the next generation. God is excised from our schools and court decisions; but in tragedy our leaders invoke His Name to comfort the bereaved. And yet the Lord stands at our sides and weeps over the culture of death.

Today's Challenge: Help pro-abortion people consider the love we instinctually feel toward newborn babies and ask them to honestly come to terms with how abortion can be aligned with their deepest convictions.

Feb 19

"Rend Your Hearts"
by Valerie Johnson

Rend your hearts, not your garments, and return to the lord, your God. ~ Jl 2:13

We know that the Lord is merciful and is calling us all to Him – to rend our hearts. Stretching and getting in shape might not be easy but we need to do it so we can run the race. Learning and educating about human development might not be on the easy list either but we need it to defend life from conception to natural death. We know that Christ has conquered death; so we constantly return to Him, with all of our hearts. He is the only way we can successfully finish the race through the narrow gate.

Today's Challenge: Return to Him.

"Blood Speaks"
by Becky Soske

Feb 20

You have approached Jesus and the sprinkled blood that speaks more eloquently than that of Abel. ~ Heb 12:24

The blood of Jesus speaks eloquently. Imagine walking in the midst of the fallen on a battlefield. Listen closely, the blood speaks loudly of fear, pain, death. The most horrific war in the history of mankind is being waged in abortion facilities worldwide, with millions of lives lost. God, the creator of all life, is calling on us to stand and take up this greatest of causes. The blood of Jesus does speak in eloquence over this battle, forward in faith we go.

Today's Challenge: Do not grow weary, keep putting on spiritual armor and press on to victory!

Feb 21

"Choose Love"
by Justin Weiler

The things that come from within are what defile.
~ Mk 7:15

Sinning is a personal decision that points us away from God's will. Abortion, murder, adultery, greed, malice, deceit, and wrath are morally wrong things that come out from within. To truly make a difference and bring the message of life and peace to the world, the answer is love. We need to consciously avoid evil and let love pour out of us. This love may be praying outside of Planned Parenthood, writing a politician, or offering a rosary for an end to abortion.

Today's Challenge: Love is a constant decision. Resolve to choose God's will, His love, in all things.

"Their Faith"
by Shane Kapler

Feb 22

When Jesus saw their faith, He said to the paralytic, 'Child, your sins are forgiven.' ~ Mk 2:5

Jesus forgave another man's sins because of the faith of his friends. The implications are incredibly important for us. We live in a nation swimming in guilt. Like Abel's blood, the blood of our aborted brothers and sisters cries out to God for justice. And yet we have the ability to cry out as well – to beg God to forgive our nation's sins and unleash the grace of sincere repentance within our hearts. We must be like Moses who stood in the breach and interceded that the Lord would not execute judgment.

Today's Challenge: Jesus did not say if you fast, but when you fast. Fasting supercharges our prayer petitions. With a small fast today, unite your petitions to end abortion and for God to forgive us all.

| Feb 23 |

"Us against the world"
by Rosemary Bernth

Who is the victor over the world but the one who believes that Jesus is the Son of God? ~ 1 John 5:5

Every cartoon villain has a plan to take over the world, but then the good-natured hero swoops in to save the day. A real superhero walked the earth... Jesus Christ. He cured the sick, fed the hungry, and paid the ultimate price to save us from our sins. Planned Parenthood pretends to be a hero for women but provides lies and pain. We change hearts and minds of those seeking abortions through compassion and truth. Go and be a hero for the unborn!

Today's Challenge: Are you a victor over the world or have you been distracted by it? Find time today to put Christ in the center of your heart.

"Test the Spirits"
by Dr. Rich Reich

Feb 24

Every spirit that does not acknowledge Jesus does not belong to God. This is the spirit of the antichrist that is already in the world. ~ 1 Jn 4:3

The spirit of the antichrist is recognizable because it refuses to acknowledge Jesus. The abortion industry refuses to acknowledge the presence of an unborn child, and they usually do not allow a mother to see the ultrasound image that may convince her to choose life. Be on guard, because the spirit of the antichrist is already in the world. We are urged to test the spirits to see whether they belong to God, because many false prophets have gone out into the world.

Today's Challenge: Avoid the wickedness and snares of the devil. Test all spirits by their relationship to Jesus.

Feb 25

"Culture of Love"
by Fr. Andrew Dickinson

If anyone says, 'I love God,' but hates his brother, he is a liar; for whoever does not love a brother whom he has seen cannot love God whom he has not seen. ~ 1 Jn 4:20

We live in a romantic world that makes love seem light and easy. But that affection is an invitation to love, it is not love itself. Love is shown in the fullness of living, not just in the affection. To build a culture of life, we must build a culture of love. To love is to choose the good of another, even when it is difficult. Love when it hurts, love when it isn't easy, love when it is messy. We build a culture of life one loving action at a time.

Today's Challenge: Prepare your heart for great acts of love and create empathy for those who struggle to love the unborn.

"The Truth"
by Shane Kapler

Feb 26

Just as you heard that the antichrist was coming, so now many antichrists have appeared. ~ 1 Jn 2:18

The Church has been persecuted by many antichrists to the point of martyrdom. However, clinging to the truth has always allowed God to bring about a new birth, like portrayed in the fictitious movie, *The Book of Eli*. As it was in the beginning, so it will be in the end. "In the beginning was the Word... what came to be through Him was life, and this life was the light of the human race; the light shines in the darkness, and the darkness has not overcome it."

Today's Challenge: After reflecting upon your activities to advance the culture of life, ask the Holy Spirit to indicate to you how you can best serve.

Feb 27

"The Rock"
by Doug Young

Be my rock of refuge, a stronghold to give me safety.
~ Ps 71:3

There is comfort in knowing there is a safe haven in which to shelter from the storm. This rock can be at Mass or in the confessional; safely inside the walls of a pregnancy help center; or on the other end of a phone call when times are tough. But this takes courage and action. Be inspired by all those faithful Christians who have helped you seek the rock. They encouraged you, prayed with you, sacrificed themselves for you as part of the body of Christ.

Today's Challenge: Think of someone who has been there when you were seeking the rock of refuge. Reach out to them with a card, letter, email, text or phone call. Then ask God to inspire you to be there for someone.

"Mother of the Living"
by Bonnie Sabin

Feb 28

The man called his wife Eve, because she became the mother of all the living. ~ Gen 3:20

Mary is the new Eve. The hearts of Adam and Eve became divided by sin; the hearts of Jesus and Mary are perfectly united. In their self-giving, Christ becomes the revelation of the Father's love and Mary becomes the mother of the living. But in the modern age there continues a war against the woman and her offspring. Women reject childbearing; men reject the responsibility of fatherhood; we deny the fatherhood of God and the incarnation of His Son. We must go forth with our Pro-Life faith to the world.

Today's Challenge: Let us not be content with isolation or too much comfort.

Feb 29

"What is the cost?"
by Diane Overmann

I obey the command of the law given to our ancestors through Moses. ~ 2 Mc 7:30

Yes, we are Pro-Life, we are anti-abortion. What does it cost us? Are we using our voices to proclaim that all human life is sacred and injustice is not an option? There is no option when it comes to the fundamental dignity of the human person. It is not optional to value the sacred in all humanity from conception to natural death. We cannot make it an option. Lord, help us to obey your command and stand up for life.

Today's Challenge: Wear your REMEMBER The Unborn jersey in unity with thousands of teammates world-wide!

"Spiritual Sluggishness"
by Bishop Paprocki

Mar 1

I am sending an angel before you, to guard you on the way and bring you to the place I have prepared. ~ Ex 23:23

The greatest obstacle to ending abortion is sloth. Spiritual sluggishness refuses the joy that comes from God. This capital sin creates a void at the center of our being that we try to fill with transitory rushes of pleasure. Such vices never leave us satisfied and lead us to despair. The devil uses the despair to tempt us to doubt our ability to fight abortion effectively. We need the help of our Guardian Angels, to lead us and to guard us from the onslaughts of the evil one.

Today's Challenge: Let's pray. All-powerful and all-loving God, we praise you for your goodness and the gift of your creation. Help us to do our best in defending life!

Mar 2

"Not in vain"
by Dr. Patrick Castle

Shine like lights in the world, as you hold on to the word of life, so that my boast for the day of Christ may be that I did not run in vain. ~ Phil 2:15-16

Running a mile in under four minutes was one of athletics' greatest milestones. The first person to break this seemingly impossible barrier was Roger Bannister in 1954. Since then, over 1,000 people have broken the 4 min barrier because they believed and worked tirelessly, including LIFE Runner Alan Webb, who broke the American record in 2007 (3:46). We can cross the finish line that ends abortion, believe it. Invite others to join LIFE Runners for one more step, one more mile, one more life. We do not run in vain.

Today's Challenge: Imagine a world free of abortion and then run towards that reality.

"Compassionately Convicted"

by Fr. Jonathan St. Andre

Mar 3

But Yours, O Lord, our God, are compassion and forgiveness! ~ Dan 9:9

Is it possible to be absolutely convicted about the call to protect the unborn and yet to be compassionate towards those who uphold a right to aborting children? The Gospel would tell us a resounding yes. We can show compassion for our brothers and sisters because our love towards them does not mean an attitude of indifference to the tragic decision they are promoting. We don't agree with them, but we love them as a person. This is the true measure of our identity as Christians. Lord, please help us to be compassionately convicted.

Today's Challenge: Pray for a person who is against the Pro-Life position. Ask the Lord to draw them closer to Himself.

Mar 4

"Ignoring God"
by Beth Bubik

"Behold, I have prepared my banquet and everything is ready; come to the feast." Some ignored the invitation and went away. ~ Mt 22:3-4

The world is so busy. The Lord invites us time after time to the feast. Sometimes, our minds are so filled with a list of to-do items that we barely hear Christ's invitation. The Lord needs us to help others to the feast. Consider your local abortion facility workers. Pray for them. May they feel Christ's grace and mercy through us today and turn their hearts toward God.

Today's Challenge: Invite someone to the feast. Let's pray that we can save many tiny hearts by the conversion of big hearts. Jesus, we trust in You.

"Spirit of Adoption"
by Daria Monroe

Mar 5

For you did not receive the spirit of slavery to fall back into fear, but you received the Spirit of adoption. ~ Rom 8:15

Through the selfless love of God, we experience an adoption that washes us clean of our sins, sets us up as joint heirs with Christ, and frees us from the bondage of fear. This seals us to God with a loving trust that allows us to cry out "Abba Father!" With adoption comes an assurance that you are not a mistake. Though there are unplanned pregnancies, there are no unplanned adoptions. We have been sought, rescued from hopelessness, and adopted at a great price into God's family.

Today's Challenge: Take some time to reflect on His word and remember that you are adopted, loved, and valued by the God of creation.

Mar 6

"Faith in Action"
by Paul Westendorf

Jesus sent them out two by two and gave them authority over unclean spirits. ~ Mk 6:7

This is a clear example of Jesus' expectation for us to be a people of action. He wants us to go out and be seen; to be an example of His love, caring, and forgiveness to the world. If we do not act, if we do not journey out and be visible, we are saying the atrocity of abortion is ok. Let us consider then how we may spur one another towards love and life. Jesus in His infinite wisdom knew His disciples would face difficulties and should work together. He knew that getting to Heaven is a team effort.

Today's Challenge: Let us love, not in word or speech, but in truth and action.

"Least or Greatest"
by Grant Fenske

Mar 7

Whoever breaks one of the least of these commandments and teaches others to do so will be called least in the Kingdom of Heaven. But whoever obeys and teaches these commandments will be called greatest in the Kingdom of Heaven. ~ Mt 5:19

Every choice has a positive or negative consequence. Our free will can lead us to have an abortion or cause someone to have an abortion. The consequence is a lifetime of painful regret. Almost all of post abortion mothers eventually admit to regretting their abortion. Our Lord in His mercy allows us to reconcile with Him and ourselves. Life is precious, let us protect the unborn, and may the choices we make lead us to eternal life in the Kingdom of Heaven.

Today's Challenge: Do you strive to follow our Lord's commandments in all that you do? Do you take time to teach others about God's love?

Mar 8

"Disorder to Order"
by Dr. Rich Reich

In the beginning, when God created the heavens and the earth, and the earth was without form or shape, with darkness over the abyss and a mighty wind sweeping over the waters. ~ Gen 1:1-2

Scientists understand that the universe naturally moves from order to disorder. This is the second law of thermodynamics. However, God is not natural; He is supernatural. "He is not the God of disorder but of peace." The culture of death that surrounds us is disordered. It is a culture that views the killing of innocent unborn children as a contraceptive choice and assisted suicide as an act of mercy. Our culture is not going to naturally change to an ordered state. The transition from disorder to order is only possible through the power of God.

Today's Challenge: Pray for the transformation of hearts for those who do not value the dignity of all human life from conception to natural death.

"Joy of the Gospel"
by Fr. Daren Zehnle

Mar 9

Go and take your place in the temple area, and tell the people everything about this life. ~ Act 5:20

The angel of the Lord told the Apostles to go into the public square and proclaim without fear the passion, death, and resurrection of Jesus Christ. This task of speaking openly and clearly of the Good News of salvation is the mission of every man, woman, and child who has been baptized. Speaking of Jesus' love for all people is not always easy; our pride often keeps us quiet as we worry about what others will think of us. Those who are considering aborting their child and those who have already done so need to hear the joy of the Gospel in our words and see it in our lives.

Today's Challenge: Seek out one person to whom you can bring the joy of the Gospel to give them hope in the midst of strife.

Mar 10

"Cheers!"
by Dale Bartscher

I set before them the gospel. But I did this privately to those who seemed to be leaders, for fear that I had run my race in vain. ~ Gal 2:2

The apostle Paul experienced fear and doubted his calling. He overcame this with God and the help of encouraging believers. In 1954, Roger Bannister, at age 25, became the first person to run a mile in under four minutes. The 2,000-strong crowd in Oxford, England, went wild as he crossed the finish line. Did the cheers from the stands make a difference that day for Roger Bannister? Yes, indeed. We are better together as we fight for the sanctity of life!

Today's Challenge: The deceiver will try to instill fear and doubt into your life. Stay encouraged by spending time with God and fellow believers.

"Run to your Savior"
by Dr. John Sturm

Mar 11

A good shepherd lays down his life for the sheep.
~ Jn 10:11

In confronting the lies of abortion, we know that truth will overcome all attacks, so run without fear towards our Savior and scatter the wolves. As St. Francis de Sales said, "As long as life lasts, run after your Savior. But run ardently and swiftly, for what will it avail you to follow Him if you are not so happy as to reach Him?" Let us run then so as to win. May we strive to remain in union with God in all ways.

Today's Challenge: Pause and remember the thousands of children aborted today. We remember.

Mar 12 — "For the Least of These"
by Janice Todd

Truly, I say to you, as you did it to one of the least of these My brethren, you did it to Me. ~ Mt 25:40

God, our Father, exhorted us to listen to his Son, Jesus, at the transfiguration when He said, "This is my Son, My chosen; listen to Him!" Our Blessed Mother Mary, reiterated that exhortation at the wedding at Cana when she said, "Do whatever He tells you." Jesus states clearly what we are to do. We are to be merciful to others - to feed the hungry, give drink to the thirsty, welcome the stranger, clothe the naked and visit the imprisoned. Indeed, all these acts of love and mercy are fulfilled as we stand up for the least of these, the unborn, and offer help to mothers and fathers afraid of motherhood and fatherhood.

Today's Challenge: May we do for them what we would do for Jesus, Himself, so we may one day hear the glorious words, "Come, O blessed of my Father, inherit the kingdom prepared for you from the foundation of the world."

"Our Father"
by Stephanie Kemp

Mar 13

This is how you are to pray. ~ Mt 6:9

The Our Father is the most perfect prayer and the summary of the whole Gospel. The Catechism says it is a path that leads directly to the heart of God. Because of this prayer that Jesus taught us, we have the confidence to call God, our Father. Jesus, who has called us into relationship with Himself, grants us this privilege by the grace of our adoption. He has made us sons and daughters of God, and He calls each of us by name. What's in a name? For post-abortion mothers, naming their child is often the difference between a life haunted by despair and one of restoration with God.

Today's Challenge: Pray for the tens of millions of walking wounded mothers and fathers who chose to abort their children… may they join us in praying, Our Father.

Mar 14

"God Grows"
by Matt Laugeman

Therefore, neither the one who plants nor the one who waters is anything, but only God, who causes the growth. ~ 1 Cor 3:7

Remain in the Spirit. Every day when you wake, be mindful of our Lord's presence, and be ready to answer His call. In all that you do, realize that it is the Holy Spirit that produces the good fruits of our labors. Brothers and sisters do not be discouraged if the secular world does not accept what we give. All we can do, as God's co-workers, is plant and water. God will cause the growth in His time, not ours. Have faith in the One who created us. He is the divine author and in control.

Today's Challenge: Start your day off with a sincere prayer, "Here I am Lord - send me!" Christ's love, through you, can save lives.

"Multiplication problem"
by Dr. Rich Reich

Mar 15

But they said to Him, 'Five loaves and two fish are all we have here.' ~ Mt 14:17

As Christians, we can feel overwhelmed by the cultural meltdown that is taking place with family, marriage, sexuality, and the dignity of human life. The apostles seemed overwhelmed. How were they going to feed over five thousand people? Jesus was able to take their gifts and multiply them for the benefit of many. It is a daunting task to evangelize a culture that does not respect the dignity of all human life from conception to natural death. Do not be overwhelmed. Jesus will multiply our gifts and feed many.

Today's Challenge: Give your limited resources and watch God multiply your efforts.

Mar 16

"Breath of Life"
by Joe Hourigan

God formed man out of the clay of the ground and blew into his nostrils the breath of life, and so man became a living being. ~ **Gen 2:7**

God breathed life into us… and counts every conceived baby as one of His children. The momentum has swayed in favor of a culture for life because of Pro-Life movies like Blood Money and Maafa21, news about Planned Parenthood's institutional evil, and the great number of young people standing up for life. But still, much work remains. We need people that are not just willing to die for the cause, but to live for it. Continue spreading the message of life-giving love.

Today's Challenge: Consider praying at least monthly outside your local abortion facility. This is like praying at the foot of the cross… expect to be blessed and converted closer to the heart of Christ.

"Parent's Greatest Gift"
by Dr. Kevin Vost

Mar 17

What father among you would hand his son a snake when he asks for a fish? If you then, who are wicked, know how to give good gifts to your children, how much more will the Father in Heaven give the Holy Spirit to those who ask Him? ~ Lk 11:11,13

Despite our fallen natures and proneness to sin, we want good things for our children. But what then is a parent's greatest gift? That greatest of gifts, of course, is life. It starts with a literal gift of one's self, as God gives the Holy Spirit. It was simply common sense in the days Jesus walked the earth, that parents would not ever give their child something deadly. How then today can parents think it wise to give to a child in the womb the instruments of abortion?

Today's Challenge: Pray with your children… this is a very good gift.

Mar 18 — "Trying to see Jesus"
by Doug Young

Herod said, "who is this man about whom I hear such things?" ~ Lk 9:9

Herod kept trying to see Jesus. In truth, Jesus is present in the person next to us, the person behind us, in front of us, and in the persons with whom we live and work. Where do we get the power to love Jesus in others? St. Mother Teresa wrote, "To be able to love one another, we must pray much, for prayer gives a clean heart and a clean heart can see God in our neighbor. If now we have no peace, it is because we have forgotten how to see God in one another." Through prayer we will receive the grace to see others with the mind of Jesus.

Today's Challenge: See Jesus in one person today, and then do something loving for them.

"Step Out"
by Dr. Rich Reich

Mar 19

Lord, if it is really You, tell me to come to You across the water. ~ Mt 14:28

Peter got out of the boat and started to walk toward Jesus on the water. Only when he started doubting did he become afraid and begin to sink. We must trust and have faith in Christ who strengthens us. We must venture out of the boat to defend the dignity of all human life in our homes, communities, and on the sidewalk at abortion facilities. Keep your eyes on Jesus and you will not falter. He will always sustain you!

Today's Challenge: Be courageous! Wear your "REMEMBER The Unborn" jersey as a public witness in unity with our thousands of teammates around the world. This will give others courage to step out of the boat and defend the dignity of all human life.

Mar 20 — "Love Your Unborn Neighbor"
by Deacon Sam Lee

You shall love your neighbor as yourself. ~ **Rom 13:9**

The reason we shouldn't kill unborn children is because we ourselves shouldn't be killed. The reason we help pregnant women in need is because we should be helped when we are most vulnerable. The reason why we have respect for the elderly, the infirm, the disabled and the forgotten is that we should be respected when we are old, sick, incapable or ignored. Pope Francis stated: "Even the weakest and most vulnerable, the sick, the old, the unborn and the poor, are masterpieces of God's creation, made in His image, destined to live forever, and deserving of the utmost reverence and respect."

Today's Challenge: Challenge yourself to look at others and imagine you are looking in a mirror. Find a way to exercise sacrificial love toward a neighbor today.

"Speak Life"
by Shane Kapler

Mar 21

Jesus was driving out a demon, and when the demon had gone out, the mute man spoke and the crowds were amazed. ~ Lk 11:14

The United States proclaims liberty and extols human rights, and yet denies the most fundamental right - that of life - to millions of its children. Our nation is rotting from the inside, and if it refuses to turn from this path it will eventually collapse. Jesus drives a mute demon out of a man so he can speak truth. May we use our voices to protest and pray. We pray that the stronger man binds the evil of abortion and exorcises it from the hearts and minds of our nation.

Today's Challenge: Petition Jesus to drive the mute spirit out of our nation, so we speak up for the least of these and save We The People.

Mar 22

"Mighty Champion"
by Carol Cooper

The Lord is with me, like a mighty champion. ~ Jer 20:11

Jeremiah deals with the struggles of speaking openly about his belief in God. The persecutions are overwhelming, and yet the fire of God's love burning within him is too strong; he has to let it out; he has to share it, no matter the consequence. Jeremiah's humble struggle is such an inspiration to us in our struggle to protect life. It is inevitable that at some point we will encounter despair, but Jeremiah reminds us that if we praise and thank God always, entrust our cause to Him, and seek to serve His will at all times, He will bring good out of all things.

Today's Challenge: Go to a chapel and kneel before Jesus and repeat over and over, "I love you, Lord, you are my strength."

"Fowler's Snare"

by Bridget VanMeans

Mar 23

We escaped with our lives like a bird from the fowler's snare. ~ Ps 124:7

How often do we really consider that if it weren't for the grace of God and Christ's work on the cross, our souls would've been hopelessly doomed. Each of us has been rescued from the fowler's snare. Now we must embrace a sense of immediacy and expectancy that God is doing something through us to bring abortion to an end… not in a generation, or a decade, but today in our sphere of influence. This sense of the now must dramatically alter the way we speak, pray, and behave in our life saving mission.

Today's Challenge: Are your petitions to God aligned with His extraordinary nature? Pray big. Pray for an end to abortion.

Mar 24

"The Ultimate Protection"
by Stacey Wollman

Jesus prayed, "Holy Father, keep them in Your name, so that they may be one just as we are one. ~ Jn 17:11

Serve the Lord with confidence! He is praying for us. It is vitally important to remember that Christ is the reason we share truth, hope, and love to those facing an unexpected pregnancy. As Jesus prays for us, we pray for mothers who walk into abortion facilities and pregnancy help centers. It is our privilege to be caring, compassionate, and truthful. We leave the results to the Lord. Every day, we witness the love of God in action. Our identity is in Christ.

Today's Challenge: Don't be discouraged. We are partnering with the living God. Act and rest in Jesus.

"Messengers for Life"

by Dr. Patrick Castle

Mar 25

Behold, I am sending My messengers ahead of you.
~ Lk 7:27

LIFE Runners carry their "REMEMBER The Unborn" jersey message for the least of these. What we do for the least of these we do for Christ. John the Baptist was a messenger for Christ - the Way, the Truth, and the Life. John the Baptist leaped in Elizabeth's womb when Mary and unborn baby Jesus drew near. Yes, unborn baby John the Baptist recognized unborn baby Jesus. Thank you for answering God's call to be a messenger for life!

Today's Challenge: Go to liferunners.org, join the team, and wear your "REMEMBER The Unborn" jersey as a public witness for the least of these. Running optional, faith required. Like John the Baptist, let's be a messenger for God's gift of life.

Mar 26

"Den of Thieves"
by Angi Castle

My house shall be a house of prayer, but you have made it a den of thieves. ~ Lk 19:46

The den of thieves looks glamorous in pop culture and tempts us every day. We must stand up to the den of thieves in our homes, schools, and churches. The den of thieves is responsible for pro-death thinking that rationalizes abortion. For example, while rape is a violent and tragic act, the mother should not be subjected to an additional act of violence that further victimizes her and her unborn child. Abortion in cases of rape heaps violence upon violence and robs the mother of a glimpse of light in a dark situation.

Today's Challenge: We need to be uncomfortable in our Pro-Life battle if we want to be heard. Stand up for the dignity of all human life from conception to natural death... and be uncomfortable.

"Prayer Matters"
by Mary Grabosky

Mar 27

Take nothing for the journey, neither walking stick, nor sack, nor food, nor money, and let no one take a second tunic. ~ Lk 9:3

God will care for all of our needs and will lead us on our uniquely designed path if we stay close to Him in prayer. Prayer also changes hearts and moves mountains. We must do our part and be warriors of prayer for the unborn. No matter where we are or what we are doing, each moment of our day, all our work, and every movement can be a prayer offered up to change the hearts of those who do not see the simple truth that life begins at conception. We live as a prayer to defend those in the womb.

Today's Challenge: Choose some moment or situation today to offer up as a prayer for the sanctity of all life, from conception until natural death.

Mar 28 — "Religious Liberty"
by Bishop Robert Gruss

Then repay what belongs to Caesar to Caesar and to God what belongs to God. ~ Mt 22:21

We enjoy freedom in America because all are created equal, endowed by our Creator with certain unalienable Rights - the right to life and religious freedom. Religious liberty, the most cherished of freedoms, is being eroded. When people are hindered from professing and living their faith, human dignity is offended. Faith plays a critical role in working for the common good of all. We must intensify our prayers and fasting for a new birth of freedom so that life and liberty is granted for all, born and unborn.

Today's Challenge: Each voice spoken to our political representatives can make a difference. This is how we bring the light of the Gospel to public life. Let your voice be heard!

"Engage for Change"
by Paul Westendorf

Mar 29

He gave them ten gold coins and told them, 'Engage in trade with these until I return.' ~ Lk 19:13

As Christians it is our responsibility to engage our neighbors and build a community of love, faith, and respect for life. We must speak out against injustice and engage for change! History shows that evil intentions can only succeed when those of good do not act. With abortion we are face to face with the greatest evil of our time. It is not enough to say, "I wouldn't have an abortion but what others do is up to them." We are called to invest in a life of love and faith that helps the least of these.

Today's Challenge: Avoid the comfort of silence. Engage your neighbors with truth to build a real community of love.

Mar 30 — "Speaking Truth & Life"
by Pastor Don Bird

Herod feared John, knowing that he was a righteous and holy man. ~ Mk 6:20

John spoke directly to the injustices of the religious elites and government authorities. John's courage came from his knowledge that his life was preparing the way for our Messiah. John's courage inspires us to speak to the injustice of abortion and the consequences it has on families and society. As those who follow Christ, we are Christ-bearers in the world. We advocate for the life of the unborn, we love the abortion vulnerable mothers, we reach out to the post-abortion mothers, we work toward strengthening the life-fabric in our society – and we do it all in His name.

Today's Challenge: Prepare yourself now for the next opportunity to speak truth and life into the dark and dying corners of our world.

"Filled with the Spirit"
by Amy Kosta

Mar 31

When the Advocate comes He will testify to me. And you also testify, because you have been with Me. ~ Jn 15:26-27

Christ sent the Holy Spirit to bring wisdom and courage to His apostles so they could proclaim His words without fear. We, too, are called to testify to Jesus; He who is the Way, the Truth and the Life. Jesus wants His Pro-Life disciples in the current culture of death to stand strong to advocate for the most helpless of all human life. We have the Holy Spirit to keep us strong. Let us go forth to walk, run and testify for all human life.

Today's Challenge: Ask the Holy Spirit to give you the courage to give witness to life for another.

Apr 1

"Step into the Light"
by Karen Patnaude

But even if our Gospel is veiled, it is veiled to those who are perishing, lest the light of the Gospel should shine on them. ~ 2 Cor 4:3-4

When brought into the light, you can come to a place of conviction, which leads to repentance, forgiveness, and peace with salvation through Jesus Christ. Women who have had an abortion need to let God heal them. They need to know that there is forgiveness in Jesus. They need to know that we all have sinned which requires repentance. Before someone knows God they are enslaved by sin. It is our job to speak truth, bring them into the light, and help them anchor to God's laws for real freedom.

Today's Challenge: Pray for God to give you opportunities to reach out to those who need to hear the truth, and then be boldly obedient as God leads you.

"Giving it all"
by Jeff Grabosky

Apr 2

If you wish to be perfect, go, sell what you have and give to the poor, and you will have treasure in Heaven. Then come, follow Me. ~ Mt 19:21

This man lived a life that followed the commandments but had a difficult time parting with his many possessions. God has given each of us certain gifts and we are called to use those gifts in a manner that demonstrates we seek the Kingdom of Heaven rather than the temporary riches of the world. Everything we have, whether it is wealth, time, talent, or especially life itself, is given to us by God. Let us today and everyday be willing to give it all back to Him.

Today's Challenge: To demonstrate that we seek first the Kingdom of Heaven, wear a LIFE Runners "REMEMBER The Unborn" jersey as a public witness.

Apr 3 — "Looking Back"
by Scott Casmer

To what shall I compare the people of this generation? We played the flute for you, but you did not dance. We sang a song for the dead, but you did not weep. ~ Lk 7:31-32

Imagine you are an archaeologist many years from now attempting to determine what life was like in the late 1900s and early 2000s. One might be baffled to explain a culture that had unprecedented material abundance and medical knowledge yet chose to kill millions of healthy unborn children. This generation accepted abortion as a choice and promoted it through government programs. What could have driven them to place such a low value on human life? What actions can we take today to keep this from being our legacy?

Today's Challenge: Start a conversation about the dignity of life from conception to natural death - encourage, pray, fast.

"Not judging sin is sinful"
by Dr. Rich Reich

Apr 4

Stop judging, that you may not be judged. ~ Mt 7:1

The past couple generations have misconstrued this verse to mean that we should not judge sin. Pro-abortionists often say that they would not choose abortion, but that we have no business interfering with the right of others to have an abortion. Permitting abortion when you fully understand that it destroys a human life and wounds the parents is a sin. It is the sin of permissiveness. We hate the sin. We love the sinner. Permitting a woman to abort her child is not love, but the selfishness of apathy or cowardice.

Today's Challenge: Fight apathy by loving those affected by abortion. Fight cowardice by standing up against abortion.

Apr 5

"Recognize Him?"
by Kathy Castle

He saw the city and wept over it saying, 'If this day you only knew what makes for peace – but now it is hidden from your eyes.' ~ Lk 19:41-42

Jesus wept for Jerusalem who turned away and did not recognize Him. Do we recognize Christ in our midst? A retreat, daily prayer, Mass attendance, Eucharistic adoration, a newborn baby's cry, a beautiful sunset - all help us recognize Him. Surely our Lord weeps for the world as He sees innocents aborted by the millions. God reminds us that even if a mother forgets her child, He will not forget us. Jesus has not forgotten us, but will our nation recognize Him?

Today's Challenge: Skip lunch and go to Eucharistic adoration once a week. Be ready to be amazed! God is calling us to a spiritual transformation.

"Kingdom Divided"
by Steve Castle

Apr 6

Every kingdom divided against itself will be laid waste and house will fall against house. ~ Lk 11:17

The Catholic Church is criticized for its unwavering, uncompromising defense of human dignity and life. The world calls for a more progressive Church. One willing to redefine marriage; celebrate abortion; show mercy for the terminally ill; and allow the destruction of embryos for stem cell research. Others demonize the Church through its scandals, dwindling church attendance, and cite the hypocrisy from within. As Christians we know there will be a separation of the goats from the lambs. What remains of the Church in this culture war will be a holy remnant, undivided, and tested by fire.

Today's Challenge: Do not waiver from the principles of human dignity and life.

Apr 7

"New Generation"
by Ann Schaefbauer

Anyone who gives you a cup of water to drink will surely not lose his reward. ~ **Mk 9:41**

Do you know someone who is thirsting for God? Give them a cup of His life-saving truth to drink. Our good deeds will be rewarded in Heaven. Eternally speaking, this world is but a moment and built-up treasure here is meaningless. Let's focus our lives on building treasure in Heaven. Let's work towards strengthening the resolve of the new generation to be a voice for the unborn, impacting hearts and minds for saving lives!

Today's Challenge: Pray for a resolve to be His hands, feet, and voice for Pro-Life. Pray for the courage to stand firm in your faith.

"To Do Your Will"

by Kathryn Lopez

Apr 8

To do Your will, O my God, is my delight, and Your law is within my heart! ~ Ps 40:8

Our Lord is holy, innocent, undefiled, and higher than the heavens. Jesus Christ is God. He walked our walk. But he did it without sin. We look around and see a dark fog. A changing culture. One mired in years of legal abortion. One that has lost its way. We must redirect. We do this by living sacramentally, wanting to do nothing without God. Abortion is an open, gaping wound in the heart and soul of our nation. God's love can heal this wound. We must walk and run with love. Knowing and sharing God's love. It's the cure. He's the cure.

Today's Challenge: Would they know we are Christians by our love?

Apr 9

"Encircled"
by Kathy Forck

Your enemies will raise a palisade against you; they will encircle you. They will smash you to the ground and your children within you. ~ Lk 19:43-44

By not accepting Jesus, we will be encircled by the world and become victims of abortion. With Christ, we focus on prayer for conversion of hearts; hearts that instead of seeking selfish gratification will put God and others first. We are in the midst of a battle and a palisade is being erected around us. Our religious freedom is being attacked as well as the lives of the unborn. We are in the battle of our lives and the battle for lives. Let us not grow weary of this work, and in His time, the victory will be the Lord's.

Today's Challenge: As a public witness, wear your LIFE Runners "REMEMBER The Unborn" jersey.

"Full Court Press"
by Pastor Rick Foreman

Apr 10

Forgetting what is behind and straining toward what is ahead, I press on toward the goal to win the prize for which God has called me heavenward in Christ Jesus.
~ Phil 3:13-14

Words such as "straining" and "press" depict the intentional focus needed to disconnect from our past and to connect with Christ and our calling. Much like sports, we cannot be content in playing a prevent defense, when God is calling for a full court press. LIFE Runners are stepping into that full court press, where the future is not left to happenstance. We stand on Phil 4:13, knowing that we can do all things through Christ who gives us strength. With Him, we are the change impacting our culture for life.

Today's Challenge: Are you going for broke by invading the darkness with the light and love of Jesus Christ? LIFE Runners show that going for broke tenacity to walk in love while standing for justice and influencing others for Christ.

Apr 11

"It's All God's stuff"
by Dr. Patrick Castle

All things came into being through Him. In Him was life. ~ Jn 1:3-4

Faith and science go hand in hand because it's all God's stuff. Life begins at conception - scientifically understood for decades. At the moment of conception, we have a unique human genome. We are alive! But this reality isn't enough for our culture to defend life from conception to natural death. After all, many of those who saw Jesus raise Lazarus from the dead were amazed yet didn't defend Him. Let this challenge us to share more compassion and love as catalysts to help others see and defend God's truth all around us.

Today's Challenge: When you see God's truth today, share it with others. Love others closer to God, and they will become more Pro-Life.

"Fear Blinds, Faith Sees"
by Pastor Don Bird

Apr 12

Take care, you remain faithful and do not fear; let not your courage fail. ~ Is 7:4

When we listen to fear, it can easily become a barrier to God's mission and work in the world. Fear is not of God, it blinds and paralyzes us. Christ strengthens, defines, and protects us. Let us not have little faith, but rather beg God for an outpouring of His grace to battle in the world for the least of us. Lord, give us the gift of faith in every moment of everyday. Help us to be courageous for the unborn so every soul may experience your promise of eternal life.

Today's Challenge: Let our words and actions reflect God's love for every person we encounter in our homes, communities, and at abortion facilities.

Apr 13

"Never Alone"
by Karen Nolkemper

You, Lord, will not forsake your people, nor abandon your very own. ~ **Ps 94:14**

Protecting and defending life is like running a marathon, not a sprint. Whether you've been running for 4 days or 40 years, you're never alone. God's got your back. The evil one will use fear, abandonment, disappointment and exhaustion to discourage you and distract you from the finish line. Stay focused. Some of us will serve on the front lines as sidewalk advocates and Pro-Life legislators, while others will be deployed behind the scenes as parish coordinators, youth ministers and chastity educators. Keep going, finish strong.

Today's Challenge: Remember, life will be victorious. Run this race set before you with your eyes courageously fixed on Jesus.

"Facing Ridicule"
by Deacon Bob Waller

Apr 14

I and my sons and brothers will not obey the king's words by turning aside from our religion. ~ 1 Mc 2:20,22

Mattathias and his sons turned away from a corrupt king, challenged others to remain loyal to God, and left behind all of their possessions. How many times in our lives do we take the easy path, avoiding possible criticism and ridicule from those around us in the workplace or in our social gatherings? Have we failed to defend what is right because it might cause us some loss of favor? As society attacks the sanctity of life and the institution of marriage do we remain silent? Is our commitment to our faith not strong enough to lead us to speak up and take action?

Today's Challenge: Seek above all else to know His will and to have the strength to do it.

Apr 15 — "God's Law on our Hearts"
by Scott Casmer

I will place my law within them, and write it upon their hearts; I will be their God, and they shall be My people. ~ Jer 31:33

We must be vigilant about doing the right thing, even when it's exceptionally difficult. Every day in America, thousands of children are intentionally killed in the womb with the approval, and often funding, of the government. Society says that we are to quietly accept the slaughtering of innocent lives. However, we must stand up and remind people of the tragedy that is all around us, while praying for the conversion of those who are not yet standing with us.

Today's Challenge: Look around and find an item near you. Imagine 3,000 of those items. Perhaps it is 3,000 bricks on a wall in front of you. Think of each of those bricks as a precious life, part of a beautiful cathedral, the Body of Christ!

"The Answer Is Love"
by Lauren Muzyka

Apr 16

This I command you: love one another. ~ Jn 15:17

Many debate in the Pro-Life movement about the best tactic for ending abortion. It is love. Love is what led Christ to the cross to redeem all sin and death, and love raised Him from the dead. Love is what heals relationships, transforms broken hearts and gives us the ability to persevere and do what's right. When we love abortion-vulnerable mothers with prayers and assistance, their hearts can be transformed and lives saved. Christ can work miracles through us, if we let Him.

Today's Challenge: Invite a friend to go with you to an abortion facility this week and peacefully pray, even if just for 15 minutes. Consider getting trained as a sidewalk advocate.

Apr 17

"True Fatherhood"
by Dr. Patrick Castle

Your opponent the devil is prowling around like a roaring lion looking for someone to devour. ~ 1 Pt 5:8

The Devil seeks to devour true fatherhood. God built men to protect their families. When the Titanic sank over 100 years ago, history was rightfully ashamed of the privileged men who took life boat seats from women and children. Men led women and children to the gas chambers in the Nazi concentration camps, and men are now coercing mothers into taking the lives of their own children at abortion facilities. Most abortions are coerced, primarily by men who discourage choosing life by saying something or nothing at all, silence is consent.

Today's Challenge: Men, bring abortion vulnerable women to pregnancy help centers, not abortion facilities. Men need to love women and their children.

"Images of Life"
by Dr. Rich Reich

Apr 18

And the chief priests plotted to kill Lazarus too, because many of the Jews were turning away and believing in Jesus because of him. ~ Jn 12:10-11

The plot of the chief priests to remove the truth of Lazarus' existence reminds us of how the abortion industry tries to prevent mothers from seeing the ultrasound image of their unborn child, the truth of their child's existence. The abortion industry knows that most women who see their baby by ultrasound choose life. The ultrasound allows the mother to realize that the decision she is making involves the life of another human being, a life that God has entrusted her to nurture.

Today's Challenge: Help reveal the truth to others. Support pregnancy help centers that provide free ultrasounds for mothers so that they may see their child and choose life.

Apr 19

"Life wins!"
by Pastor Don Bird

Do not be afraid. ~ Mt 28:10

We are a voice of life and hope in the world. Refuse to be shackled by fear, overtaken by darkness, and imprisoned by death. We live our lives in such a way that we point the Way to our living God. God is Pro-Life, He is all life. And, because He is life, we are not to fear, even when we are confronted by suffocating darkness and the sting of death. The resurrection of our Lord gives us the freedom and the joy to remind a deceived world of the sacredness and miracle of life. Life wins!

Today's Challenge: Write a text, email, and social media message that shares about the sanctity of life from conception to resurrection.

"Speak Life"
by Alice Chapman

Apr 20

That I may know how to sustain the weary one with a word. ~ Is 50:4

There are many voices joining in the life debate. Some are calm and loving, some are angry and scornful. Some lay out thought-provoking rationale, and some simply provoke divisiveness and rage. Each of us is positioned to speak truth and rouse awareness to those who need to hear the message. We should gently, persistently share the truth where and when we have the opportunity. God has given us well-trained tongues and will supply us with words to speak to the weary.

Today's Challenge: Look for an opportunity to share an encouraging or instructive word to someone in your circle of influence.

Apr 21

"Who are You?"
by Sara Beaner

I do know Him and keep His word. ~ Jn 8:55

Do you know Jesus and the people near you? Do others know you? Who are you? Hopefully, a follower of Jesus, a loyal defender of all life from conception to natural death, and a disciple giving Christ's love to all. Rejoice and be glad for we know Jesus, the Son of God, who chose to suffer and die for our sins. He is the love and mercy that will end abortion.

Today's Challenge: Take time to share your love of Christ with your family, neighbors, and friends.

"The Father's Mouthpiece"
by Dr. Rich Reich

Apr 22

I say only what the Father has taught Me. ~ Jn 8:28

Jesus told us what the Father taught Him. He arose early to listen to His Father and to pray to Him. As disciples of Christ, we imitate Him in all that He does. Because Jesus spent much time listening to the Father, so do we. The Father will teach us what to say. When you are confronted with defending your faith and your Pro-Life beliefs, take comfort in knowing that the Father will speak through you.

Today's Challenge: Be brave in defending your faith.

Apr 23

"Take our Hearts"
by Amy Kosta

The Lord is close to the brokenhearted; and those who are crushed in spirit He saves. ~ Ps 34:18

As advocates for life, our goal is to reach the hearts of those facing crisis pregnancies as well as those families who have been hurt by the lies of abortion. We are reminded that the Lord is right beside us in this effort. Just like Jesus, we are called to reach out to women in trouble or distress. We are called to support expectant mothers through encouragement, guidance, and continued contributions to pregnancy help centers. We are called to provide healing support to anyone hurt by the tragedy of abortion.

Today's Challenge: Stay close to the brokenhearted, those hurt by abortion, so they may find peace and healing.

"Have Mercy on Us"
by Mary Grabosky

Apr 24

The Lord is compassionate and gracious, slow to anger, abounding in love. ~ Ps 103:8

We look at the ways of the world and see the blood of the innocent being shed. It is understandable that our Father in Heaven has wrath. The Lord said to Moses, "I see how stiff-necked this people is. Let me alone, then, that my wrath may blaze up against them to consume them." At this Moses implored the Lord to not allow His wrath to blaze up against His people and our Lord in His mercy relented. Let us ask our Father in His mercy to remember us as we pray and work to end abortion.

Today's Challenge: Pray that the Lord will have mercy on us.

Apr 25

"Blue Angels"
by Ed Heigl

My soul proclaims the greatness of the Lord; my spirit rejoices in God my Savior for He has looked with favor on His lowly servant. From this day all generations will call me blessed. ~ Lk 1:46-48

Mary is the perfect example of faith and trust. Like John who leapt in the womb when Mary arrived, we need to leap into action to defend life. The Navy's Blue Angels help protect lives. LIFE Runners are Blue Angels for the voiceless unborn and their families. The Blue Angels are powered by jet fuel. We are powered by the grace of our Lord Jesus Christ who has "The Right Stuff" for eternal life.

Today's Challenge: Read Psalm 45 and then pray for all of those involved in the business of abortion, including our executive, legislative, and judicial leaders.

"Actions Speak"
by Angi Castle

Apr 26

Preach the gospel so that the cross of Christ might not be emptied of its meaning. ~ 1 Cor 1:17

Meditate on the crucifix. Imagine the pain suffered throughout the body of Christ with thousands of lives lost every day to abortion. Jesus' actions spoke louder than His Words. We wear our LIFE Runners jerseys with the simple yet powerful message, "REMEMBER The Unborn." It is a message that causes contemplation and action. It is a message that brings dignity and hope. We look at Christ crucified and remember the powerful life-saving meaning of the cross. As St. Francis of Assisi implores, let us preach the gospel at all times and if necessary use words.

Today's Challenge: Reflect on the cross that Christ carried for us. May this inspire us to more often carry the "REMEMBER The Unborn" jersey message on our backs for the least of these.

Apr 27 — "Knit In Our Mother's Womb"
by Dr. Kevin Vost

Truly You have formed my inmost being; You knit me in my mother's womb. ~ Ps 139:13

God knit us in our mother's womb. He knows us and loves us perfectly. "Behind and before you encircle me and rest your hand upon me." Each of us was once encircled, encompassed within our mother's wombs, while God knitted us into being by His love. Our mothers lovingly rested their hands upon their swollen bellies that encircled us. May the words of this psalm inflame our souls and inspire us to serve and protect every child that God so carefully knits.

Today's Challenge: Share the love of Christ with one person today.

"Bystanders"
by Dr. Patrick Castle

Apr 28

Live in a manner worthy of the call you have received.
~ Eph 4:1

Our culture is filled with bystanders who didn't intervene while abortion ended millions of lives. These bystanders consider themselves pro-choice but not pro-abortion, which isn't logical because abortion is one of the choices they support. This is reflected in the fact that about half of Americans identify as pro-choice, but more than half consider abortion morally wrong. Pro-Life bystanders think their lack of participation in abortion is enough to be Pro-Life. Silent bystanders actually speak loudly. Many abortions happen because a mother interprets silence as consent. Most post-abortion women said they would have chosen life if just one person had intervened with support.

Today's Challenge: Don't be a bystander to abortion. Speak up with support that encourages abortion-vulnerable mothers to choose life. Be the one!

Apr 29

"Household of God"
by Paula Parmalee

You are no longer strangers and sojourners, but are fellow citizens with the holy ones and members of the household of God. ~ Eph 2:19

Before legalized abortion, most people simply didn't or couldn't conceive the thought of babies being killed in the womb. The news of Roe v. Wade was the landmark decision and defining moment when human life became disposable. We became acutely aware of the preciousness and sacredness of life. A heightened sense of the supernatural took a firm grip on us. This is a battle of principalities, a spiritual battle far greater than we alone can overcome. We are "fellow citizens with the holy ones." We are living the New Evangelization professed by St. John Paul II. We must step forward to profess the Gospel of Life with boldness, charity, and love.

Today's Challenge: Step out of your comfort zone and reach out to abortion vulnerable women in your community.

"Be-Attitudes"
by Scott Casmer

Apr 30

Join with others in being imitators of Me, brothers and sisters. ~ Phil 3:17

By being Pro-Life, we strive to imitate Christ. There are people who seek to discredit our efforts. We need to be vigilant about our behavior. We need to love as Christ loves. He tells us to love our neighbor. Others notice our LIFE Runners jersey, "REMEMBER The Unborn" car magnet, Respect Life license plate, baby feet pin, and crosses. If they observe contrary behavior, it raises doubts about all we support.

Today's Challenge: Embrace the LIFE Runners Be-Attitudes: be Christ-like, be prayerful, be Pro-Life, be respectful, be charitable, be peaceful.

May 1

"Save What Was Lost"
by Jeff Grabosky

For the Son of Man has come to seek and to save what was lost. ~ Lk 19:10

Zacchaeus was a wealthy tax collector, a person rejected by the people due to the nature of his business. Jesus seeks out Zacchaeus as well as all sinners and the lost. There are times in my life when I was counted among the lost. We can take confidence in knowing Jesus is always seeking us out and all we have to do is open our hearts to Him. We are called to be Jesus to others in the same way He reached out to us. We should reach out to those who may be lost, and especially reach out in any way we can to those who may be considering an abortion. In doing so, we allow Jesus to work through us in bringing the lost back to Him.

Today's Challenge: Look for someone today who might be among the lost and reach out to them in the same way Jesus would.

"Be Strong"
by Pastor Rick Foreman

May 2

Praise the Lord in His sanctuary, praise Him in the firmament of His strength. ~ Ps 150:1

We need to be strong and courageous as LIFE Runners to protect the unborn. The importance of meditating on God's word and activating it out on a daily basis is paramount to engaging His power source for strength and courage. The Bible clearly states that death and life are in the power of the tongue. In our efforts to promote God's agenda, are we being strong and courageous in speaking the truth in love?

Today's Challenge: Study scripture. "In the beginning was the word, and the word was with God, and the word was God Himself."

May 3

"Thanks Always"
by Stephen Schmidt

Let all Your works give You thanks, O Lord. ~ **Ps 145:10**

Most of us can easily think of many things for which we are thankful; family, friends, a warm home, plenty of food… life itself. It is more difficult, however, to give thanks to God when we are beset with troubles; an illness, loss of a job, loss of a loved one. It can be challenging to be thankful for the ministry opportunities with abortion workers, but these are incredible moments to share the love of Christ. We are called to embrace God's will in every moment! God has a plan for every soul, not to do harm but plans to give us hope and a future.

Today's Challenge: Look for God in all things and all occurrences in your life; especially in the mundane. He is always working!

"Hanging on Words"
by Peggy Bowes

May 4

The leaders of the people, meanwhile, were seeking to put Him to death, but they could find no way to accomplish their purpose because all the people were hanging on His words. ~ Lk 19:47-48

Jesus is with us when we pray at abortion facilities because we are gathered in His name. Allow Him to speak through you. Pray that those who are seeking to put babies to death will find no way to accomplish this because of His words spoken by us. Pray the LIFE Runners Creed to end abortion. Trust that Jesus will use your prayers to impact hearts and minds for saving lives!

Today's Challenge: Ponder the words a Holocaust survivor shared: "Never be silent whenever and wherever human beings endure suffering and humiliation. Always take sides! Neutrality helps the oppressor, never the victim. Silence encourages the tormentor, never the tormented."

May 5

"Sights and Sounds"
by Diane Overmann

They that hope in the Lord will renew their strength, they will soar as with eagles' wings; they will run and not grow weary, walk and not grow faint. ~ Is 40:30-31

So many years have passed since God sent the message to Isaiah to tell us to hope in the Lord. As we experience our darkest time, and the world's most grievous sin, may we choose to believe in the light. I choose to believe that abortion will end. Peace will come as the King of Glory comes and the nations rejoice. I am one small voice saying "I believe." Please join me.

Today's Challenge: Wear your "REMEMBER The Unborn" jersey as a public witness in unity with our thousands of teammates.

"I Will Help You"
by Lisa Skowron

May 6

For I am the Lord your God who takes hold of your right hand and says to you, 'do not fear, I will help you.'
~ Is 41:13

My relationship with God was restored through a post-abortion Bible study. It was the hardest thing I had ever done. As I processed the fear, anger, and grief with God, the healing began. God's love and peace overwhelmed me, and I found freedom from the shame and sorrow I had carried for so many years. It was a profound experience of His grace, and I finally understood the power of Christ's sacrifice on the cross for me. I was forgiven! I pray for post-abortion women to know how God can take their deepest pain and heal it. Christ will not abandon or betray anyone. He is a gentle and loving Savior.

Today's Challenge: The anger and denial at the abortion facility is from deep pain and shame. Show them God's love, which will draw them to the light.

May 7

"God's Goodness"
by Dr. Kevin Vost

You anoint my head with oil; my cup overflows. ~ Ps 23:5

Christ heals the mute and the deformed and the lame and the blind before he performs the miraculous multiplication of the loaves and the fish. The Christian knows that all life is good and valuable. We hear it several times in Genesis when God declares what He made was good, indeed, very good, and when He commanded His creatures to multiply and fill the earth. Let's think of those precious babies that were made by God for union with Christ. Let's do what we can to heed God's call to be fruitful and to value and protect every single life. May every human being share in the abundance of good things that He intends.

Today's Challenge: Let's raise our hearts and minds today to request from God that our nation will return to the unyielding defense of the inalienable right to life.

"Alpha and Omega"
by Peter Kahama

May 8

"I am the Alpha and the Omega, the Beginning and the End," says the Lord God, who is, and who was, and who is to come, the Almighty. ~ Rev 1:8

The hope of humanity is depressed, and the fear of death has taken root. Where in our life are we depending on hope? Who is our hope? Our Lord God is the Alpha and Omega who has all that we need. Let nothing stop you from preaching this hope. When faced with difficult moments, like avoiding abortion or healing from abortion, turn to Him, the giver of all life and hope!

Today's Challenge: Share your experience of God's life-giving hope with at least one person today.

May 9

"Spirit of God"
by Dr. Kevin Vost

Those who keep His commandments remain in Him, and He in them. ~ 1 Jn 3:24

Christ commanded us to love one another. If we are to act according to the Spirit of God, we must love every unborn child by allowing them life, a gift that we all have been given. In that same spirit of love, we will love and support the parents who choose life despite the difficulties and obstacles they feel. Our love must also extend to the mothers and fathers who were sold the abortion lie, supporting them with the Spirit of God for healing.

Today's Challenge: Pray for those wounded by abortion to choose healing and life. Many abortions are repeat abortions. See stats at liferunners.org/represent.

"Clear the Fog"
by Dr. Rich Reich

May 10

This is the time of fulfillment. The Kingdom of God is at hand. Repent and believe in the gospel. ~ Mk 1:15

Sometimes our eyes are too clouded by the fog to see God's presence, but He is powerfully present within us. The dense fog can contain our worries, shame, envy, and pride. The remedy is clearly stated in the Gospel, "repent and believe." The Son clears the fog with His forgiveness when we repent. Then we can see Him present in the depths of our heart. Women experiencing unplanned pregnancies sometimes find themselves in a fog of despair. Be the guiding light for these women. Lead them to the peace that only our loving and forgiving Father can provide.

Today's Challenge: Allow the Son to clear the fog. Repent and believe in the gospel.

May 11

"Endure Suffering"
by Scott Casmer

Remember the days past when, after you had been enlightened, you endured a great contest of suffering. ~ Heb 10:32

Doing the will of God requires us to endure suffering at times. Even a simple conversation about abortion with friends and co-workers can lead to an emotionally charged debate. Persons who publicly witness the truth of abortion through marches, sidewalk advocacy, and wearing LIFE Runners gear often experience the jeering of those who do not understand that the value of human life trumps all other causes. The discomfort we experience must be endured with firm conviction that the end goal is well worth it. "The truth is like a lion; you don't have to defend it. Let it loose; it will defend itself."

Today's Challenge: Watch a Pro-life movie like *Unplanned*. This movie devours the lies of abortion.

"Such a Time"
by Lisa Skowron

May 12

Ask and it will be given to you; seek and you will find; knock and the door will be opened to you. ~ Mt 7:7

Esther then went before God in complete humility, asking for His guidance and revelation. Risking her own life, but knowing God was with her, Esther went before the King without being summoned. Haman's plot was foiled and turned against him, and the Jewish people were saved. We must go before the Lord in humility, asking for His guidance and seeking His will for us in helping to end the abortion holocaust of our day. Using Esther as our example, let us witness with love, patience, kindness, humility, and peace. May we all be a people called "for such a time as this."

Today's Challenge: Wear your "REMEMBER The Unborn" jersey as a public witness to impact hearts and minds for saving lives. Post photos with #RememberTheUnborn.

May 13

"Mother of God"
by Dr. Sebastian Mahfood

A great sign appeared in Heaven: a woman clothed with the sun, and the moon under her feet, and on her head a crown of twelve stars. ~ Rev 12:1

Our Lady of Guadalupe is an image that contains another image – that of the unborn Christ still in her womb as can be seen from the black wrapping around her upper waist, a sign of her pregnancy. While clothed by the sun and with the moon under her feet, Mary presents to us not only all of creation as we know it but also the begotten God who has revealed himself to us in the person of Jesus Christ. Wrap yourself in the love of Mary, a woman whose choice was life!

Today's Challenge: Allow the grace of God to work through you to love every mother and father tempted to abort their child and offer healing support for post- abortion parents.

"Bad For Business"
by Dr. Rich Reich

May 14

The unclean spirits came out and entered the swine. The herd of about two thousand rushed down a steep bank into the sea, where they were drowned. ~ Mk 5:13

Jesus sent the unclean spirits from a possessed man into a herd of swine, and the two thousand swine rushed down a steep bank into the sea and drowned. The swine-herders believed that their personal profits were more important than the possessed man's welfare. Planned Parenthood believes that Pro-Lifers are bad for business, especially when we pray and advocate for the well-being of the mothers, families, and unborn children affected by abortion. Like the swine-herders, they are more concerned about personal profits than the welfare of mothers and their children. Help others see that people are more important than profits.

Today's Challenge: Show your commitment to life by praying and advocating for the mothers, families, and unborn children vulnerable to abortion.

May 15

"Remedy For A Sore Loser"
by Jeff Grabosky

Let your life be free from love of money, but be content with what you have, for He has said, I will never forsake you or abandon you. ~ Heb 13:5

We are reminded today to love one another and be content with what we have, keeping in mind what is most important – the treasure of Heaven. God tells us repeatedly that He will never abandon us. This does not mean we will sail through life without any problems. Remind those whose hearts are shattered by abortion that it is often in our suffering that we draw closer to Him. God is faithful, generous, and loves us more than we can ever comprehend. As we battle to end abortion, let us have confidence that He will never abandon us.

Today's Challenge: The next time you feel like getting frustrated or sad over some type of loss, offer a prayer to God thanking Him for being with you through the challenge.

"Life Scars"
by Abby Johnson

May 16

The Lord is close to the brokenhearted. ~ Ps 34:18

Many of us in the Pro-Life movement are scarred by abortion in some way. Every time I go to an abortion facility to pray and do sidewalk advocacy, I am reminded of my two children that I aborted. I am also reminded of the thousands of children who were killed on my watch. I am reminded of the blood on my hands. But more than anything, I am reminded that I am forgiven. Praise God for His mercy! I thank God for my life scars. God can use all of us to minister to others, no matter what we have experienced in our life. Praise God that He can turn our sins and hurt into His glory!

Today's Challenge: Don't fear your hurt. Use it to help others. Let Christ heal your heart and your grief. Let Him work a miracle in your life.

May 17

"Like Father, Like Son"
by Dr. Kevin Vost

Amen, amen, I say to you, the Son cannot do anything on His own, but only what He sees the Father doing; for what He does, the Son will do also. ~ Jn 5:19

Christ powerfully reminds us that God is a Father and Jesus Christ is His Son. As Jesus Christ sought only to please His loving Father in all that He did, so should we. As the Father loves the Son, so too should every earthly father and mother also love every single son and daughter that springs forth from their union. Let us pray that every child will be allowed to live and will come to know the love of a father and a mother, so that sons may desire to be like their fathers, and daughters to be like their mothers.

Today's Challenge: Pray for the unborn that they may live to know the love of a father and a mother.

"Faith Precedes Miracles"
by Dr. Rich Reich

May 18

He and his whole household thereupon became believers. This was the second sign that Jesus performed.
~ Jn 4:53-54

Faith precedes miracles. In John's Gospel, seven miracles are recorded "to help us believe that Jesus is the Messiah, the Son of God, so that through this faith we may have life in His name." Jesus disapproves of faith as merely an effect and makes it primarily the cause. He rebukes the people: "Unless you people see signs and wonders, you do not believe." A life devoid of faith will result in a life devoid of miracles. As LIFE Runners, we need to have faith in the eventual end of abortion. We run to end abortion, for Christ has destroyed the power of death, and therefore the power of abortion.

Today's Challenge: With faith that Christ is working through you, be generous with your time, talent, and treasure today.

May 19

"Healing Support"
by Dr. Patrick Castle

It was in the name of Jesus Christ the Nazorean whom you crucified, whom God raised from the dead; in His name this man stands before you healed. ~ Act 4:10

The healing power of Christ is in all of us. With the millions of abortions, we have many healing opportunities around us. May we have the courage to reach out to post-abortion women compassionately. Keep taking steps in your "REMEMBER The Unborn" jerseys. Imagine those first few steps out of the upper room when the Apostles went out to evangelize the whole world. With the power of the Holy Spirit within us, we are taking steps to heal and elevate our culture to respect life from conception to eternity.

Today's Challenge: When sharing the reality of abortion with others, deliver the truth with compassion as someone listening is likely suffering from the regret of choosing abortion.

"Fighting God"
by Scott Casmer

May 20

But if it comes from God, you will not be able to destroy them; you may even find yourselves fighting against God. ~ Act 5:39

The Sanhedrin wanted to punish the Apostles for publicly sharing the word of God. They were charged with being false prophets. Gamaliel warned the rest of the Sanhedrin that it may be best not to punish them because if the Apostles were doing God's inspired work then the Sanhedrin would be fighting God. Those who fight against the Pro-Life movement are fighting against God. Let's meet our lost brothers and sisters with compassion and love them to the Pro-Life side, welcome them to our team, God's team.

Today's Challenge: Compassionately educate those who may be unknowingly fighting against God. Life facts can be found at liferunners.org/represent.

May 21

"Passover Supper"
by Diane Overmann

This day shall be a memorial feast for you, which all your generations shall celebrate with pilgrimage to the Lord, as a perpetual institution. ~ Ex 12:14

Every act of love proceeds from the Pascal mystery and brings the Kingdom more present in our world. At the Last Supper, the Passover meal, Jesus reminds us of the time when God freed His people from slavery. Now we have modern slavery: media, consumerism, and the culture of death. In the garden, Jesus asked His friends to watch with Him for one hour. Let us recommit ourselves to watch with Him for one hour each week at abortion facilities. What does Jesus see as He stands outside an abortion facility?

Today's Challenge: Will I hunger with Jesus to feed both the child vulnerable to abortion and the mother who is a slave of her fears?

"God and Country"
by Bonnie Sabin

May 22

Remember not against us the iniquities of the past; may Your compassion quickly come to us, for we are brought very low. ~ Ps 79:8

There has been a call to prayer and fasting many times in our country, the first in 1775 by the Continental Congress and notably in 1863 by President Lincoln. Psalm 79 expresses our nation's position before God. "Let the prisoners' sighing come before you; with your great power free those doomed to death. Then we, your people and the sheep of your pasture, will give thanks to you forever." We are indeed prisoners by the affliction of abortion and our sin. Let us be the sheep of His pasture and let God lead us to victory over abortion.

Today's Challenge: Take the next step in your walk with God. Go beyond your current comfort level.

May 23

"Deserted Places"
by Fr. Daren Zehnle

I was provoked with that generation. ~ **Heb 3:10**

As God was provoked with that generation who rebelled against Him in the desert, we too may be provoked with our generation. Our provocation will sometimes lead us to disdain and disgust with those whose hearts are hardened against life. We must be wary in our zeal to defend the dignity and beauty of all human life, lest we too, harden our hearts. When we are provoked with our generation, we must follow the example of Jesus.

Today's Challenge: When speaking with a person who supports abortion, let us seek to lovingly show them the truth and lead them to the Savior.

"Difference Makers"
by Dr. Patrick Castle

May 24

Though I thought I had toiled in vain, yet my reward is with the Lord who formed me as His servant from the womb. ~ Is 49:4-5

While praying at abortion facilities, we compassionately meet the confusion going in and the hurt coming out. "An old man was walking down the beach. He saw a boy picking up stranded starfish and throwing them back in the sea. As the old man approached, he asked, "Why do you spend so much energy doing what seems to be a waste of time?" The boy explained that the stranded starfish would die if left in the sun. The old man exclaimed, "But there must be thousands of starfish. How can your efforts make any difference?" The boy looked down at the starfish in his hand and as he threw it to safety in the sea, he said, "It makes a difference to this one!""

Today's Challenge: Let's remember the story of the starfish and be the one to reach out to an abortion-vulnerable woman.

May 25

"Go That Extra Mile"
by Dr. Rich Reich

Should anyone press you into service for one mile, go with him for two miles. ~ Mt 5:41

No one likes to be made to do someone else's work. At the very least, we are apt to complain, argue, or simply refuse to be so used. But Jesus tells us to carry such a burden an extra mile. Pro-Lifers hope to convince the abortion vulnerable mother that carrying the pregnancy to term is the best choice for both the baby and the mother. This is true, but what about the mother after the pregnancy? The mother will need just as much support after the pregnancy as she did during the pregnancy. This is where we are called by Jesus to go that extra mile. Our job is not over when the baby is born.

Today's Challenge: Support Pro-Life programs that help the mother and child before and after pregnancy.

"Change Us"
by Ed Heigl

May 26

Jesus said to those Jews who believed in Him, 'If you remain in My word, you will truly be My disciples, and you will know the truth, and the truth will set you free.'
~ Jn 8:31-32

I lost my one and only older sister to abortion. My mother's pain from her choice to abort my sister remained with her the entire 96 years of her life. It's a shame that so many people accept the toxic scourge of abortion which has become a holocaust many times larger than what happened in Nazi Germany. They lack respect for the human person. I had family members who were prisoners in Nazi concentration camps because they stood up for life. It is time that we allow God to work through us, so we can protect the least of these and set the captives free.

Today's Challenge: Stand up and speak up for life! Wear your "REMEMBER The Unborn" jersey as a public witness, raising awareness and letting the truth of abortion set our world free.

May 27

"Heaven Is A Team Effort"
by Dr. Patrick Castle

Therefore, I say to you, the Kingdom of God will be taken away from you and given to a people that will produce its fruit. ~ Mt 21:43

Heaven is a team effort, and LIFE Runners are "a people that will produce its fruit." A cross country team fields seven runners but only five count towards the final score. The two extra runners are there to help push the first five forward. However, at the finish, all seven runners are recognized for the result, the fruit produced. We need all LIFE Runner teammates to pray and move towards the finish line that ends abortion. Our life-saving teamwork produces fruit to feed a culture of life, All In Christ!

Today's Challenge: Every day let us strive to plant, water and wait patiently for God to make our efforts grow.

"Be Rich Soil"
by Dr. Patrick Castle

May 28

And some seed fell on rich soil and produced fruit.
~ Mk 4:8

LIFE Runners plant seeds of truth with our "REMEMBER The Unborn" jersey message wherever we go. We water those seeds with love, compassion, service, and prayer. God causes growth when our efforts reach rich soil. The great commandment is to love God with all our heart and to love our neighbor as ourselves. The more we love God and our neighbor, the more Pro-Life we become. To be Pro-Life is to be filled with a JOY - Jesus, Others, You - that prompts us to put our live-saving faith in action for others. We pray that our jersey message finds rich soil, allowing God to impact hearts and minds for saving lives!

Today's Challenge: Plant lots of seeds today by inviting others to join our team. Water those seeds by praying the LIFE Runners Creed.

May 29

"Blessed Are We"
by Dr. Patrick Castle

Jesus said, many prophets and kings desired to see what you see, but did not see it, and to hear what you hear, but did not hear it. ~ Lk 10:24

Blessed are the LIFE Runners who see and hear the goodness of the Lord and act on it. Simply desiring God is not enough, we are called to reach out to God through our service to neighbor. Acts of faith transform our desires into a living faith. Sidewalk advocacy provides so many opportunities for acts of faith. Jesus said that whatever we do for the least of these, we do for Him. Therefore, in the form of prayers and service, let us be a light for the unborn, elderly, foster children, handicapped, homeless, prisoners, post-abortion mothers, and others seriously wounded by sin.

Today's Challenge: Purchase food gift cards to give out to the homeless. This is safer than giving cash and handy when asked at stop signs.

"My Yoke"
by Mary Grabosky

May 30

Come to Me, all you who labor and are burdened, and I will give you rest. For My yoke is easy, and My burden light. ~ Mt 11:28,30

Our burdens and sufferings, when united to Christ, are beautiful gifts when offered for others. Christ also tells us that He gives strength to the fainting; for the weak he makes vigor abound and will renew their strength. Let us unite our burdens to Christ and offer them for those men and women that may be pondering abortion. Let us pray that they will find hope in the Lord, and He will renew their strength.

Today's Challenge: Pray the Our Father for the men and women who may be considering abortion right now.

May 31

"Lip Service"
by Dr. Rich Reich

He said in reply, 'Yes, sir,' but did not go. ~ Mt 21:30

Jesus asked the opinion of the chief priests and the elders of the people, "Who did his father's will?" One son said "no" to working in the vineyard, but then he changed his mind and went. The other son said "yes", but did not go. Do we give "lip service" to Jesus by saying yes to God's will, but then do nothing? The message is clear; what pleases God is not our obedient words, but our obedient actions. Pregnancy is a "yes" to loving a child but sometimes the "yes" in faith becomes a "no" out of fear, leading to abortion.

Today's Challenge: Say "yes" to God today and then back up your "yes" with obedient actions.

"To Everything Is A Season"
by Pastor Rick Foreman

Jun 1

There is an appointed time for everything. And there is a time for every event under Heaven. ~ Ecc 3:1

A.W. Tozer once said, "When you kill time, remember that it has no resurrection. So many people in society today are living as if the purpose of life is to arrive safely at death." Even Benjamin Franklin stated, "Most people die at 25 but are not buried until 75." Yet as Christians, we have already died to ourselves in order to live for Him and take the message of life to others. As LIFE Runners, that time is to not allow today's complacency to become tomorrow's captivity. We need to use the time we already have differently.

Today's Challenge: Be intentional in praising God constantly.

Jun 2 — "Tender Compassion of God"
by Angi Castle

In the tender compassion of our God, the dawn from on high shall break upon us, to shine on those who dwell in darkness and the shadow of death, and to guide our feet into the way of peace. ~ Lk 1:78-79

In the tender compassion of God, our Savior Jesus Christ was born in a humble stable. He shines upon all who live in darkness and the shadow of death. Mary knew He was our light in the darkness; she risked much to carry Christ in her womb. May we reflect upon our many blessings and pray for those who are struggling to find their way out of the darkness – those contemplating abortion. May that innocent baby born in a manger, that crisis pregnancy, help keep us focused on ending abortion with peace and love.

Today's Challenge: Pray for those working at abortion facilities who are lost in the darkness.

"Fish Story"
by Dr. Rich Reich

Jun 3

Come after Me and I will make you fishers of men.
~ Mt 4:19

The first thing that Andrew did after meeting Jesus was to seek out his brother Simon and tell him that he had found the Messiah. With his first cast, Andrew caught not just a man, but the fisher of men and women, Simon Peter. What a fish story! Andrew, on his first try at evangelism, caught the man who would later catch three thousand on the day of Pentecost. Who are you called to tell about Jesus today? Have you invited them to our faith in action LIFE Runners apostolate? Have you neglected to share because of laziness or fear? Do not put it off for another moment.

Today's Challenge: Be an Andrew today and spread the word about our life-saving apostolate, LIFE Runners.

Jun 4 — "Run with Endurance"
by Finau Leggett

Therefore, since we have so great a cloud of witnesses surrounding us, let us also lay aside every encumbrance and the sin which so easily entangles us, and let us run with endurance the race that is set before us. ~ Heb 12:1

We need to live a holy and transformed life in Christ to maintain our endurance in the race. In Christ we can do all things, in making a stand for Christ in a world that is infested with worldly compromise, pleasing man and unholiness. Our cause to defend the unborn and support families to make right decisions should never be shaken. Also, we are grateful to our fellow Christian family members who urge us on to complete our race. For in our different gifts and talents, we compliment and build each other up in grace, endurance and love.

Today's Challenge: Help someone join the LIFE Runners team today. liferunners.org/join

"The Law of Human Dignity"
by Fr. Jonathan St. Andre

Jun 5

For you did not receive a spirit of slavery to fall back into fear, but you received a spirit of adoption, through which we cry, 'Abba, Father!' ~ Rom 8:15

Jesus kept the religious law of His time and honored the sabbath, but He recognized the law's role as helping the human person flourish. A good law respects the basic rights and dignity of the human person. So, in this case, blessing the woman's life was greater than enforcing a law for a law's sake. When our culture can see in human persons the inviolable God-given right to life, then we are on the way to true life.

Today's Challenge: Take five minutes to pray for every soul to recognize the value of every human life, and to prioritize protecting all life from conception to natural death.

Jun 6

"A Mother's Cry"
by Dr. Rich Reich

Jesus said to His mother, 'Woman, there is your son.' In turn He said to the disciple, 'There is your mother.'
~ Jn 19:26-27

Jesus presents the care of His mother to His disciple. We are all disciples of Christ and have the responsibility of taking care of mothers in need. With the pro-life ministry, sometimes all of our passion goes toward saving and protecting the unborn child and sometimes we forget about the mother in need. When we turn our focus to the mother and her needs, she will be encouraged to choose life for her unborn child.

Today's Challenge: Be sensitive to the needs of every mother.

"Follow Me"

by Dr. Rich Reich

Jun 7

As He moved on, Jesus saw a man named Matthew at his post where taxes were collected. He said to him, 'Follow Me.' ~ Mt 9:9

Like the apostle Matthew, we sense something inside our hearts calling us to service. We have heard His calling and donned our "REMEMBER The Unborn" jerseys as a public witness in defense of the unborn. It has never been popular to follow Jesus, nor to be Pro-Life, but Jesus is calling us to do so. To be Christ's disciple means becoming a fool in the eyes of the world, just as many would believe that we are foolish to get involved with a woman's decision to have an abortion. As God tells us over 300 times in the Bible, do not be afraid.

Today's Challenge: Be like Matthew; follow Christ in the defense of the unborn and lead others to also follow Him.

Jun 8 — "Prayer Warrior"
by Mary Grabosky

He said to them, "Take nothing for the journey, neither walking stick, nor sack, nor food, nor money, and let no one take a second tunic." ~ Lk 9:3

God will care for all our needs and will lead us on our uniquely designed path if we stay close to Him in prayer. Prayer changes hearts and moves mountains. We must do our part and be warriors of prayer for the unborn. No matter where we are or what we are doing, each moment of our day, all our work, and every run or walk can be a prayer offered up to change the hearts of those who do not see the simple truth that life begins at conception, and that all lives have immense value. As LIFE Runners, "we run as a prayer to defend children in the womb." Let us pray!

Today's Challenge: Choose some moment or situation today to offer up as a prayer for the sanctity of all life from conception until natural death.

"Greatest in the Kingdom"
by Alice Chapman

Jun 9

Whoever becomes humble like this child is the greatest in the Kingdom of Heaven. And whoever receives one child such as this in My name receives Me. ~ **Mt 18:4-5**

We are called to approach our Heavenly Father with the unabashed awe and trust of a child. Jesus helped His disciples to understand that it is only when they stopped measuring their importance by society's standards and recaptured child-like faith, that they could truly begin to experience the Kingdom of God right here on earth. Jesus also tells us that receiving and loving a child in His name is like receiving Him! Every child is like a little piece of Heaven and has infinite value. Sidewalk advocates help bring more of Jesus into this world that so desperately needs Him.

Today's Challenge: Commit to taking just 5 minutes each morning to reconnect with God in prayer and recapture the child-like faith within you.

Jun 10 — "Expect Nothing"
by Bernadette Costello

Nor did we seek praise from men, either from you or from others. ~ 1 Th 2:6

We are called to think, speak, and act out of love for God. Why do you choose the church you attend, the people you serve, or the place that you pray? Is it to fulfill something inside of you, or is it out of love of God and neighbor? As sidewalk advocates, we meet broken-hearted, hopeless, and lost souls. We cannot effectively love and bring them to Christ if we are doing it out of love of self. It is only by God's grace and our surrender to Him, that we can bring light to the darkness of abortion. Do whatever He tells you because you love Him, not because of anything else.

Today's Challenge: Spend some time with God today without any distractions.

"Don't Give Up"
by Pastor Don Bird

Jun 11

And for this reason we too give thanks to God unceasingly that, in receiving the word of God from hearing us, you received it not as the word of men, but as it truly is, the word of God. ~ 1 Th 2:13

Paul offers encouragement to those in Thessalonia to continue to allow God to work through them. When the word of God is the center of our lives, it generates within us the desire and willingness to engage in life-giving activity. I encourage you not to give up. Continue in the labor of love as you do your part in building a culture of life. When His word lives in you, the life and light of Christ shines through you.

Today's Challenge: Take time to find God's encouragement through His word and pray that His word may lead and guide your steps to bring life and light everywhere you go.

Jun 12 — "Strangers In Our Own Land"
by Amy Kosta

Amen I say to you, no prophet is accepted in his own native place. ~ Lk 4:24

We are strangers in our own land! The battle against the culture of death is painful. We must accept rejection and continue to witness for life as Christ does, with kindness and love. We must wear our LIFE Runners blue proudly, move with conviction, and pray that the Lord will soften those hearts hardened by the culture of death.

Today's Challenge: Say a special prayer for those who have rejected you because of your Pro-Life convictions. Pray that God might soften their hearts to see every human life as a reflection of His glory.

"The Fast Track"
by Dr. Rich Reich

Jun 13

Before Jesus had finished speaking to them, a synagogue leader came up. ~ Mt 9:18

Jesus was talking about a new way of living and fasting. He then resurrected the little girl, and immediately following that, healed the hemorrhaging woman. These miracles of healing and resurrection are put in the context of Jesus' words on fasting. The key to the power of fasting lies in self-denial. Indeed, self-denial is essential to following Christ. As followers of Christ, may we be an example of self-denial in our time given to serve parents arriving at abortion facilities and pregnancy help centers.

Today's Challenge: Take the fast track and let the Holy Spirit empower you in every word you speak to abortion-vulnerable parents, so they see and hear Him.

Jun 14 — "Hardship for Heaven"
by Bernadette Costello

It is necessary for us to undergo many hardships to enter the Kingdom of God. ~ Act 14:22

It is in the darkest moments of our lives that we often surrender the most to God. Every hardship that we experience is an opportunity to become closer and more intimate with Him, which ultimately leads us closer to His Kingdom. Praise God for being called to battle for the unborn! Praise Him for all the people we encounter, all our hardships, and all the ridicule we receive in His name. Beg Him for the grace to surrender so that it is Him who speaks when we are conversing with abortion-vulnerable parents. His love gives hope, heals, and consoles every heart.

Today's Challenge: For the next nine days, commit to praying the Surrender Novena.

"May Glorify God"
by Peggy Bowes

Jun 15

I glorified You on earth by accomplishing the work that You gave me to do. ~ Jn 17:4

Think of these words of Jesus when you are standing in front of your local abortion facility in the pouring rain, freezing temperatures, or even a beautiful day when you would rather be somewhere else. You are glorifying God and doing His work through your presence as a witness for the unborn, who have no voice but ours. You are radiating Christ's love to everyone who passes by as you pray on the sidewalk. You may never know who you influence or how your prayers help, but your Heavenly Father knows and is pleased.

Today's Challenge: Try to devote one day a month to praying in front of your local abortion facility.

Jun 16

"Finish the Race"
by Dr. Rich Reich

Their wealth remains in their families, their heritage with their descendants. ~ Sir 44:11

Jesus warned us about "laying the foundation and then not being able to complete the work." The culture of death views the moral crimes of abortion and euthanasia as individual rights. "Choices once unanimously considered criminal and rejected by the common moral sense are gradually becoming socially acceptable," St. John Paul II declared. As LIFE Runners, we need to continue to persevere against the culture of death until we complete the work of ending abortion. We need to pass the baton onto the next generation, so that they can continue the work. This requires us to invest in our families and to educate people on the sacred value of life.

Today's Challenge: Support LIFE Runners who educate children about the sacred value of all life from conception to natural death.

"Keep Me Safe O God"
by Paula Parmelee

Jun 17

Keep me safe O God; in You I take refuge. I say to the Lord, You are my Lord, You are my only good. ~ Ps 16:1-2

Keep me safe, O God; you are my hope. Surely the greatest grief of all is the loss of a child by abortion. Share with others that Christ suffers every bit of their pain with them, and He weeps for every tear they shed. He hears their cries of sorrow. He is a gentle, merciful, and loving Father. Share His endless mercy with those you meet who suffer from their choice to abort their child. It is only in Christ that anyone will find healing, peace, and true joy.

Today's Challenge: Offer prayers, friendship, love, and time to a woman who has suffered the loss of her child from abortion.

Jun 18 — "Lord, I Want to Know You"
by Bernadette Costello

Then He opened their minds to understand the Scriptures.
~ Lk 24:45

So many of us seek to know Christ but neglect to spend time with Him. As St. Jerome said, "ignorance of scripture is ignorance of Christ." We can have an authentic and intimate relationship with Him right now if we spend time reading His word. God brings simplicity to our lives. In Jer 1:5, we know that God knew us even before we were in our mother's womb. This truth opens our minds to understand God's will so that we can be His mercy to abortion-vulnerable parents. It is through our support that they will come to realize God's love for them in all situations, preventing and healing abortion.

Today's Challenge: Spend 5 minutes each day reading or listening to the word of God.

"Jail Break"
by Dr. Rich Reich

Jun 19

What are you willing to give me if I hand Him over to you?' They paid him thirty pieces of silver. ~ Mt 26:15

When the apostles were set free, they obeyed God by going out and taking their place to teach in the temple, as God's angel had commanded them. Many of us are imprisoned by our shame, guilt, addictions, etc. Jesus is ready to open the gates of our jail through confession, but once free, what will we do? He will command us: "Go out now and take your place in the temple precincts and preach to the people all about this new life." Jesus frees us not only from slavery, but also for evangelization.

Today's Challenge: Ask God for the grace to stand at an abortion facility and share the good news.

Jun 20

"Let The Sun Rise"
by Mary Ellen Hoffman

Be attentive to the word, as to a lamp shining in a dark place, until day dawns and the morning star rises in your hearts. ~ 2 Pt 1:19

We must give our full attention to the word of God. It gives specific instructions of how to obtain completeness, joy, and ultimately Heaven. We can be confident that He will always bring light to the darkest situations. As the sun rises each morning, we need to open our hearts to Him and find out what great surprises He has in store for us. May we pray for those contemplating abortion that they allow God's light to open their hearts to know His love and peace.

Today's Challenge: Smile at everyone you pass by today. It will brighten their day as well as yours.

"Called to be a Servant"
by Alice Chapman

Jun 21

The greatest among you must be your servant. Whoever exalts himself will be humbled; but whoever humbles himself will be exalted. ~ Mt 23:11-12

Jesus makes it very clear that all of us are called to be servants to one another. Throughout the gospels, we see many examples of Jesus healing the sick, driving out demons, and feeding the hungry. Even though He was God and obviously had a message of salvation to bring to His people, He first showed them His great love and served their basic needs with humility. In our efforts to bring an end to abortion, we must focus on meeting the needs of abortion-vulnerable women right where they stand.

Today's Challenge: Consider simple, practical ways that you can show Christ's love to women in your community to prevent abortion.

Jun 22 — "Convincing Truth"
by Dr. Rich Reich

If they do not listen to Moses and the prophets, they will not be convinced even if one should rise from the dead. ~ Lk 16:31

The rich man from the netherworld begs Abraham to send Lazarus from the dead to warn his five brothers, so that they may not follow the path of life which led him to his place of torment. Abraham then replies that if they do not listen to Moses and the prophets, they will not be convinced by someone from the dead. Pro-Life ministry is trying to teach others the truths about abortion, but the message falls upon many deaf ears. Many times, it is not a voice from the dead that provides the convincing truth, but an ultrasound image of the unborn life within them.

Today's Challenge: Be the convincing voice of truth for those who cannot speak for themselves.

"Forgiveness is the Key"
by Dr. Rich Reich

Jun 23

My heavenly Father will treat you in exactly the same way unless each of you forgives his brother from his heart. ~ Mt 18:35

The Lord has suffered for our sins and He forgives us. Likewise, we are commanded by Jesus to forgive others. We will be forgiven in the same way that we forgive. If we do not forgive our brother from our heart, we are merely imprisoning ourselves and torturing our spirit. Forgiveness is our decision to accept God's grace to let go of offenses committed against us and to express this by acts of mercy and love. St. John Paul II defined forgiveness as "the restoration of freedom to oneself... the key held in our own hand to our prison cell."

Today's Challenge: Lead post-abortion mothers and fathers to God's forgiveness.

Jun 24

"Mind, Heart, and Strength"
by Shane Kapler

You shall love the Lord your God with all your heart, with all your soul, with all your mind, and with all your strength. ~ Mk 12:30

This is the greatest commandment given to us by God, and we are only able to love Him in that fullness by His grace. Every time that we pray the sign of the cross, we are professing our faith and obeying God's Law. By touching our forehead, chest, and shoulders, we are reminded to keep Christ in our mind and heart, so He can be our strength. Through the cross of Christ, we enter into the inner life of the Father, Son, and Holy Spirit. By grace we are empowered to do so with all our mind, all our heart, and all our strength.

Today's Challenge: Pray the sign of the cross, slowly and deliberately, three different times on behalf of the unborn and their parents.

"End of Time"
by Kevin McNicholas

Jun 25

I, the Lord, have called you for justice, I have grasped you by the hand; I formed you, and set you as a covenant for the people, a light for the nations. ~ Is 42:6

God is speaking not only to Isaiah in this verse. This is also directed to you and me. God calls us to act with justice, to devote ourselves to what we know to be "the new and everlasting covenant," and shine as a light to the nations. Our faith in God allows us not to fear anything in this world that is merely passing away. We are called to be the hands and feet of Christ, and we will never know until the end of time the miraculous impact that our Pro-Life ministry has made in the world.

Today's Challenge: Offer a prayer for a mother today, that whoever she is, she feels the real presence of Christ and chooses life!

"Presentation of the Lord"

Jun 26

by Dr. Rich Reich

Every first-born male shall be consecrated to the Lord. ~ Lk 2:23

The presentation of the first-born son was a way of remembering how the Lord freed the Israelites from slavery by killing the Egyptian's first-born. It was also an acknowledgment that God owns everything. That is part of the reason why the Lord called Abraham to sacrifice his first-born, Isaac. The Israelites offered the first fruits of the harvest to the Lord. In the new covenant, the first day of the week was offered to the Lord and called the Lord's day. When we present to the Lord our first-born, our first fruits, and our first day, we acknowledge that the Lord owns not only the first, but the last. Everything belongs to Him.

Today's Challenge: Give yourself to the Lord in service to the unborn in whatever way He is calling you to do; time, talent, and treasure.

"Why Do We Persecute Him?"

by Bernadette Costello

Jun 27

He fell to the ground and heard a voice saying to him, 'Saul, Saul, why are you persecuting Me?' ~ Act 9:4

We are all guilty of persecuting Christ. It's difficult to admit, but we are the soldiers at Calvary. Every sin we commit is another nail hammered into His flesh. Reflect on God's mercy with Saul. Even in our greatest sin, He seeks us, loves and consoles us. He lifts us high above our worth. May each of us be a reflection of His mercy to all those we meet at abortion facilities. Rejoice, and sing Hallelujah when we are persecuted for being the hands and feet of Christ.

Today's Challenge: Meditate on the crucifix today and praise God for any persecution you receive in His name.

Jun 28 — "Perfect Discipline"
by Bernadette Costello

Endure your trials as discipline; God treats you as His sons. ~ Heb 12:7

We must view our trials as opportunities to perfect the image of Christ within us. It is easy to imitate Christ with those whom we love, but God commands us to love even when it is difficult. It is crucial that we understand this. He is talking about self-giving and unconditional love. Pro-Life ministry is afforded many opportunities to imitate Christ as we encounter trials. Praise God for every trial because every trial is an opportunity to grow in holiness. Call on the Holy Spirit to give you the grace to be His instrument of love to the broken-hearted at abortion facilities.

Today's Challenge: Take time today to thank God for His clear and loving discipline.

"Narrow Road"

by Pastor Rick Foreman

Jun 29

Do not be conformed to this world, but be transformed by the renewing of your mind, so that you may prove what the will of God is, that which is good and acceptable and perfect. ~ Rom 12:2

Jesus said the gate that leads to destruction is wide and broad, many may enter it, but small and narrow is the gate that leads to life; only few find it. So many people are like the Pharisees; complacent, blind, and lacking wisdom about spiritual warfare. Abortion is the work of the demonic. May we stay close to Christ who will strengthen us and be our guide to the path of life.

Today's Challenge: Let us not let the things of this world keep us from running the race for life.

Jun 30

"Two by Two with Authority"
by Bernadette Costello

Jesus summoned the twelve and began to send them out two by two and gave them authority over unclean spirits. ~ Mk 6:7

We are created to know Christ, to love Him, and to serve Him. He commands us to go out to all the ends of the earth and preach the good news. We don't have to travel far, as abortion is taking place in our neighborhoods. Ask God to open your eyes to the demonic all around you. Plead with Him to give you the courage to go out and share His love with those who are misled and deceived at abortion facilities. Go out two by two and take authority over the demonic in His holy name.

Today's Challenge: Listen to His call today and allow yourself to be uncomfortable for Him.

"Be Fruitful and Multiply"
by Kathy Forck

Jul 1

God said, "Let the water teem with an abundance of living creatures, and on the earth let birds fly beneath the dome of the sky." ~ Gen 1:20

Countless innocent lives are lost every day due to abortion. It is everyone's responsibility to pray for our world to honor God and value the precious gift of life. Urge men to be the protector of their family; to stand up for God, baby, and self. We must always offer resources and love to families that need support. Abortion is against God in all circumstances. God said to be fruitful and multiply. Pray for yourself and your neighbor. Help build a culture of life by helping families be strong and united. Be a beacon of light to those who are in the dark.

Today's Challenge: Accept a friend's invite to pray in front of an abortion facility. Simply show up, and God will do the rest.

Jul 2 — "Blindness"
by Bernadette Costello

Do you have eyes and not see, ears and not hear?
~ Mk 8:18

The disciples' blindness made them afraid even in the physical presence of Jesus and eventually caused them to abandon Jesus on Calvary. Jesus suffers greatly because of our blindness and deafness to His words. The darkness of sin debilitates us, and we act as though we cannot see that. We must cling to Him who will restore our vision and heal our hearts. Abortion darkens the world so much that we all feel blinded and breathless at times. Allow the Holy Spirit to wash your eyes and souls so that you may wash others.

Today's Challenge: Pray about your spiritual blindness and go give the best confession of your life. The Sacrament of Confession heals and restores us.

"Two Roads"

by Fr. James Dean

Jul 3

What profit is there for one to gain the whole world yet lose or forfeit himself? ~ Lk 9:25

There are two paths that we can follow. One leads to life and the other leads to death. Choosing the path of life brings prosperity; whereas, choosing the path of death brings doom. The prosperity is not earthly. The greatest blessing is the elevation, fulfillment and glorification of the life God has entrusted to us. Jesus gives us the road map to following Him to eternal life. He said that if anyone wishes to come after me, he must deny himself and take us his cross daily and follow me. Let us pray that we are God's instruments in helping abortion-vulnerable parents.

Today's Challenge: Take one of the commandments that you have difficulty following and pray daily for the grace to be faithful to God's holy will.

Jul 4 — "Reasons for Judgment"
by Matthew Laugeman

Cry out unsparingly, lift up your voice like a trumpet blast; Tell My people their wickedness and the house of Jacob their sins. ~ Is 58:1

The great prophet Isaiah was at the right place at the right time to do the Father's will. We are all called to that same holiness, to strive to be Saints. Can our Heavenly Father count on us to do His bidding? There will always be darkness in our world until Christ returns in all His glory! Until then, we know that His light exposes everything in the dark. Brothers and sisters, when our LIFE Runners team gathers to witness for life, may God let our unity be a trumpet blast to the world.

Today's Challenge: Tell someone today about the awesomeness of God. Christ's love, through you, can change their life!

"Half Truth"
by Bonnie Sabin

Jul 5

You shall not bear hatred for your brother in your heart. Take no revenge and cherish no grudge against your fellow countrymen. ~ Lev 19:17-18

This can be extremely difficult as we encounter abortion-vulnerable parents who believe the lies of abortion. As John warns us, do not believe every spirit, but test the spirits to see whether they are from God, because many false prophets have gone out into the world. Lies about abortion and life have been told and truths twisted, resulting in so many lost souls. With understanding how careful we must be and how easily we are derailed, let us be compassionate to our brothers and sisters who fall victim to the lies of abortion.

Today's Challenge: Pray for all our lost brothers and sisters to be awakened to the truth of abortion.

"Authentic Prayer"
Jul 6
by Dr. Rich Reich

This is how you are to pray, Our Father who art in Heaven, hallowed be thy Name. ~ Mt 6:9

St. Augustine taught that the Our Father is not only a prayer, but the criterion for all authentic prayer intentions. When we say "Your will be done on earth as it is in Heaven," we are asking God to make us obedient so that His will may be done in us, as it is done in Heaven. We do not plead to change God's will but to change ourselves to accept His will. God gave us life and His will is that we have it to the fullest forever. Praying for the unborn enlightens our minds to an awareness and to a renewed conviction that all human life is sacred.

Today's Challenge: May God give us the strength to defend all human life.

"Courage and Hope"
by Diane Overmann

Jul 7

For I know the plans that I have for you, declares the Lord, plans for welfare and not for calamity, to give you a future and a hope. ~ Jer 29:11

Sometimes I find it difficult to live in the hope that the evil in our society will diminish. There are so many abortions each day. What a challenge for me to continue to stand up for what is right with renewed hope. I recall the voices of some third graders before Christmas after I shared that some people do not know Jesus. In their simplicity they announced, "Well, we have to go tell them." We must continue to stand against the evil of abortion and the degrading of human life.

Today's Challenge: Picture yourself with Jonah walking through your neighborhood announcing the call to repent.

Jul 8 — "The Victory that Conquers"
by Paula Parmelee

The victory that conquers the world is our faith. ~ 1 Jn 5:4

Faith is a gift. Jesus incarnate is the greatest gift of all. He comes into our world, our fallen humanity to free us from our sin. Yet, the sin of abortion continues to enslave and destroy lives. The victory we long for, the one that holds deepest in our hearts and desire most to embrace, is close at hand. It must first be won in our own hearts. The triumph of charity and love over hate, unforgiveness, jealousy, anger, pride, envy, and greed will reign only when our hearts are united with Christ crucified. Fortified with His love we go forth to claim victory over the world!

Today's Challenge: Reach out in love to someone you have had a disagreement with and do your part to forgive and make amends.

"Be Quiet"

by Dr. Rich Reich

Jul 9

Jesus rebuked him and said, "Quiet! Come out of him!" ~ Mk 1:25

Our culture is filled with noise. We spend so much of our time in the noises of the world that many of us struggle to spend a moment in silence. It's difficult to hear the Lord above all the noise. It is in the silence that we will find Him waiting for us. Pray, in the name of Jesus, for your mind to hush. Take time to be quiet with your family in prayerful reflection every evening. In the quiet, God asks us to help end the noise of abortion.

Today's Challenge: Spend quiet time with Jesus in adoration each week.

Jul 10

"Gift of Life"
by Pastor Don Bird

He approached, grasped her hand, and helped her up. Then the fever left her. ~ Mk 1:31

I love the healing stories of Jesus. They remind me of the purpose for which Jesus came. These miracles reveal to us the heart of Jesus and the way in which He calls us to live our lives. We identify the healings throughout the gospels as miracles, events that are beyond explanation and scientific possibility. God makes the impossible possible. Through His word or touch, light overcomes darkness, life overcomes death, despair is overcome by hope, and brokenness discovers wholeness.

Today's Challenge: Share the life and healing Christ offers with those drowning in despair at abortion facilities.

"God is Faithful"
by Amy Kosta

Jul 11

The Lord will remember His covenant forever. ~ Ps 105:8

I am reminded of how our Lord is indeed keeping His promises every time I read news of how we are winning the fight against abortion. News of laws passed imposing longer waiting periods before obtaining abortions, closing of abortion facilities, and more Pro-Life mobile units available to assist mothers to choose life are most encouraging. Of course, the fight is not close to being over. We must continue to pray for the lives of those affected by abortion. Know that the Lord will hear and be faithful to His people.

Today's Challenge: Make a special effort to pray for those who stand at abortion facilities providing sidewalk advocacy.

Jul 12 — "Answering the Call"
by Brandon McAuliffe

Jesus rebuked him and said, quiet! Come out of him!
~ Mk 1:25

I thought that I had everything in perfect order for my life to play out just the way I wanted it to when I got married in 2004, but I was wrong. I stopped attending church regularly and in just three years, the marriage was over. I ended up on the verge of suicide soon after. I felt a massive void, and nothing seemed to fill it. I prayed about what was missing in my life, and it didn't take long to get an answer. My healing began on the day that I returned to Mass.

Today's Challenge: Post-abortion mothers have increased rates of suicide ideation. Be sure to invite post-abortion mothers to church for God's healing.

"Welcome to His House"
by Stephen Holinaty

Jul 13

And inasmuch as it is appointed for men to die once and after this comes judgment, so Christ also, having been offered once to bear the sins of many, will appear a second time for salvation. ~ Heb 9:27-28

God knows that our flesh is weak, and we are only good by His grace. He will always reach out to us and hopes that we will repent and continue to strive to live a righteous life. He tells us that the righteous path is difficult, but He will remain with us always. We will always see God working once our eyes are opened. Just as God sends others to be there for us, we must open our arms to those whom we are sent to love.

Today's Challenge: Be a beacon of hope for those who suffer from the effects of abortion.

Jul 14 — "Family Divided"
by Dr. Rich Reich

Whoever does the will of God is brother and sister and mother to Me. ~ **Mk 3:35**

Jesus said that He came for division. You may find yourself divided with your family or friends on the issue of abortion. Some family members receive Him and accept His gospel of Life, and others reject Him and belong to the culture of death. Jesus offers us consolation amidst our pain. By doing the will of God, we are adopted and transplanted into the family of God. We become a member of Christ's family, united in love through the Holy Spirit. Pray for those who persecute you. Jesus is the stumbling stone that smashes a family apart and the cornerstone upon which the family is restored.

Today's Challenge: Pray for your family and friends that they may share in our respect for the dignity of all human life.

"Grace to Give"

by Kevin McNicholas

Jul 15

Those sown among thorns are another sort. They are the people who hear the word, but worldly anxiety, the lure of riches, and the craving for other things intrude and choke the word, and it bears no fruit. ~ Mk 4:18-19

It is so easy to get caught up in the attraction of worldly treasures that intrude and distract us from God. I have often thought of what I could get when I earn more money or have fewer bills to pay. Today I am going to pray for the grace to think of what I can give instead. We are not of this world but merely in it. Our salvation is all that matters. I urge you to pray for a greater detachment from things and a greater attachment to God.

Today's Challenge: Support Pro-Life ministries with your time, talent, and treasure.

Jul 16

"Why We Run"
by Chris Talley

Our great desire is that you will keep on loving others as long as life lasts, in order to make certain that what you hope for will come true. ~ **Heb 6:11**

We run as a prayer, to build endurance, for awareness, for charity… to end abortion. I have participated in several races over the years, but it was so inspiring to run with other LIFE Runners. At the finish line of a race, I was greatly impacted when a mother who saw my "REMEMBER The Unborn" jersey emotionally shared that she dedicated her race in memory of her aborted child. It was healing for her to join us and take part in our event.

Today's Challenge: Never give up in your efforts to end abortion. With Christ, life is victorious!

"Lead People to Jesus"
by Fr. James Dean

Jul 17

I do not want to send them away hungry, for fear they may collapse on the way. ~ Mt 15:32

Jesus felt pity toward those who were following Him. Jesus knew their greatest hunger was spiritual, which is why they had followed Him for three days without eating. He cured and fed them, and they continued to follow Him because they were still sick with sin and hungry for love and truth. There is still a vast crowd in the world that is sick and hungry. Jesus wants to cure and feed us all.

Today's Challenge: Be vulnerable with your testimony of God's healing and mercy with post-abortion parents. It will lead them to Him so their healing can begin.

Jul 18

"On God's Time"
by Kevin McNicholas

Then He touched their eyes and said, "Let it be done for you according to your faith." ~ Mt 9:29

God will always grant us what we need. When Jesus told the blind men let it be done for you according to your faith, it really made me stop and think about my own life. We had five years of infertility before God blessed us with two children. I learned in those five years to die to self and to trust that our timing is not God's timing. I am grateful for the time He allowed us to wait because we learned to accept His will in our lives even more. We must surrender our own wishes and desires and live in accordance with His will.

Today's Challenge: Pray for those with crisis pregnancies to accept God's plan for their lives. He will always provide what we need.

"Infinite Value"
by Dr. Rich Reich

Jul 19

If a man has a hundred sheep and one of them goes astray, will he not leave the ninety-nine in the hills and go in search of the stray? ~ Mt 18:12

Our Father in Heaven cares for all His children. He is always seeking us. One argument made by pro-abortion people is that it is acceptable to end a life, if bringing that life into the world would result in a net-negative effect to those already born. The parable of the lost sheep counters this pro-abortion lie because it clearly demonstrates that all of God's children have infinite value in the eyes of the Lord.

Today's Challenge: It does not matter if human laws have legalized the destruction of human life through abortion. Jesus teaches that we are to value every human life from conception to natural death.

Jul 20 — "Consecrated from the Womb"

by Alice Chapman

He will be filled with the Holy Spirit even from his mother's womb. ~ Lk 1:15

Expectant parents spend many hours dreaming of what their child will be like. By the time their bundle of joy arrives, they may even think they have the child's life all planned out. God reminds us that He has chosen each one of us, even before we are conceived, for a special purpose. God chose John the Baptist for the important task of preparing the people of Israel for the coming of their Messiah. Every life lost to abortion is a dream and a plan unfulfilled.

Today's Challenge: Take a few minutes today to reflect on your life's purpose, what God has planned for you. Ask Him for the grace and guidance to gently lead you there.

"Fatherless Child"
by Dr. Rich Reich

Jul 21

To turn the hearts of the fathers to their children, and the hearts of the children to their fathers. ~ Mal 4:6

A father should represent God the Father to his family. This is such a critical and irreplaceable role in a child's life that it is greatly under attack by satan and his pawns who shape the secular culture. Fathers are called to faithfully spend their lives trusting in God's provision for their family and working diligently to provide for them. It is critical that fathers protect and lead their family to Heaven.

Today's Challenge: Pray that children threatened by abortion have fathers that are willing to love as Christ loves and defend their child's life.

Jul 22

"Armor of God"
by Bernadette Costello

Take the helmet of salvation, and the sword of the Spirit, which is the Word of God. ~ Eph 6:17

I've heard many people say that "Life doesn't come with instructions" as a way to blanket their mistakes. That is not true! God gives us the perfect instruction book, the holy Bible. His love, truth, and plan for our lives are clearly stated. There's power in His words and in His holy name. He knows us better than we know ourselves. He knew us before we were formed in our mother's womb, knows our thoughts before we do, and loves us perfectly. There's no confusion about His command to love Him above all else and to love our neighbors as ourselves. Obey His commands. Support life from conception to natural death without exception. Give of your time, talent, and treasure. This pleases God and consoles His Heart.

Today's Challenge: Spend 5 minutes a day reading the Bible. This provides an intimate relationship with God.

"Love Rescues"
by Stacey Wollman

Jul 23

Let Your favor shine on Your servant. In Your unfailing love, rescue me. ~ Ps 31:16

We ask the Lord to give us favor and demonstrate His compassion as women come to find help with their unplanned pregnancy. Our goal is to present the truth by sharing with each woman that their life and the life of their unborn baby holds infinite value. That each individual human being is unique and irreplaceable. That her relationship with her child has intrinsic worth and beauty. The wonder of each mother's first glance at her child's ultrasound image brings visible truth.

Today's Challenge: Make a commitment to pray daily for abortion-vulnerable mothers to recognize their child in their womb.

Jul 24 — "Empty Yourself"
by Dr. Rich Reich

Go out to the highways and hedgerows and make people come in that My home may be filled. ~ Lk 14:23

Jesus makes room for us at His banquet. He is constantly inviting us to share in His life and longs for us to come to Him. Is there enough room for Jesus in your life, or is it too stuffed with stuff? We cannot accept Christ's invitation and be filled with Him until we empty ourselves of all the selfish and worldly distractions. Are you too full to hear His invite? I urge you to empty yourself and make room for Jesus in your life, because absolute fullness only resides in Christ.

Today's Challenge: Empty yourself to make room for Jesus, so you can share His love with abortion-vulnerable parents.

"Persevere in Faith"
by Ed Heigl

Jul 25

'Son of David, have pity on me!' Then Jesus stopped and ordered that he be brought to Him; and when he came near, Jesus asked him, 'What do you want Me to do for you?' ~ Lk 18:39-41

Life is not about being successful, rather it is about being faithful to God and to one another. Others will rebuke us for our faith and tell us to be quiet, but we must persevere. We are all beggars on the side of the road. Through His Grace and Divine Mercy, we are given the opportunity to grow in our faith and put it into action for the salvation of the whole world.

Today's Challenge: Stand up, speak out, and witness for life! If you are not already a LIFE Runner, sign up, order your "REMEMBER The Unborn" jersey and wear it proudly in public to impact hearts and minds for saving lives.

Jul 26

"Strong and Courageous"
by Pastor Rick Foreman

Praise the Lord in His sanctuary, praise Him in the firmament of His strength. ~ **Ps 150:1**

It is critical that we are strong and courageous in our journey to protect the unborn. As Christians, our confidence and solid foundation begins and ends with the word of God. Meditating on God's word is paramount to engaging the power source of strength and courage. In addition, the Bible clearly states that death and life are in the power of the tongue. In our efforts to promote God's agenda, are we being strong and courageous in speaking the truth in love? Or, do we cave to the sensitivity of those who believe contrary to the truth?

Today's Challenge: Be strong and courageous in your journey to be All In Christ for Pro-Life!

"Lukewarm"
by Bernadette Costello

Jul 27

So because you are lukewarm, and neither hot nor cold, I will spit you out of My mouth. ~ Rev 3:16

God does not need us, but He chose us. We need Him, and He hopes that we choose Him. God loves us. Are you lukewarm in your faith? Do you always stand up for life or do you stand silent when someone stands against God? God calls us to defend all life. He carefully knits each one of us in our mother's womb. He created us in His image. Call on Him to give you the grace to battle for the unborn in all circumstances.

Today's Challenge: Do not be lukewarm for Christ. Be All In Christ for Pro-Life!

Jul 28 — "Stern Love"
by Dr. Rich Reich

O stupid Galatians! Who has bewitched you, before whose eyes Jesus Christ was publicly portrayed as crucified? ~ **Gal 3:1**

St. Paul did not understand how the Galatians who have seen the image of Christ crucified, could possibly forsake Him. He did not maintain that the Galatians had misused their minds, but rather lost their minds; they had been brainwashed. This seems to be the case today with the pro-abortion movement whose arguments justifying abortion are so illogical and unscientific that only a generation of mindless people could take them seriously. If we do not crucify our flesh with its passions and desires, our carnal desires will crucify our minds.

Today's Challenge: Do not conform yourselves to this age but be transformed by the renewal of your mind. Speak the truth to others with stern love as St. Paul did to the Galatians.

"Christ Set Us Free"
by Pastor Don Bird

Jul 29

For freedom Christ set us free; so stand firm and do not submit again to the yoke of slavery. ~ Gal 5:1

Paul was disappointed at the report that though the Galatians had been growing in their faith, they were being influenced by those trying to destroy God's work of grace in them. Paul reminds them, as he does us, that the freedom we experience comes through Jesus Christ, not from adhering to rules and policies or good deeds. When we try to earn what Christ has already given, it mocks His sacrifice. We honor the work of Christ on the cross when we allow God's grace to work through us, giving us the freedom to offer grace to a world in need.

Today's Challenge: Live in the freedom that Christ offers to defend all human life, and by God's grace even the darkest corners of our world will be redeemed.

Jul 30

"Clean Hands"
by Dr. Rich Reich

But as to what is within, give alms, and behold, everything will be clean for you. ~ Lk 11:41

A pharisee, after hearing Jesus preach, invited Him to dinner because he wanted to hear more from this extraordinary man who spoke the word of God. The pharisee was offended that Jesus did not perform the ceremonial washing of hands before beginning the meal. Jesus turned the table on His host by chiding him for uncleanliness of heart. He teaches us that it is more important to have a clean mind and heart than it is to have clean hands. If the heart is full of His love, there is no room for envy, greed, or bitterness.

Today's Challenge: Give alms freely and generously to Pro-Life apostolates.

"Imitate Jesus"

by Dr. John Sturm

Jul 31

I will send to them prophets and apostles; some of them they will kill and persecute in order that this generation might be charged. ~ Lk 11:49

God sent St. Gerard Majella as a prophet to the people of Italy, so that all might know the love of God. He was ridiculed throughout his life for the degree of penance he took on himself; all in his attempt to imitate the life of Jesus. After his death, St. Gerard Majella became widely known as the saint of happy childbirth for the many miracles that he performed. Likewise, since we are running for life on God's team, we are called to imitate the life of Jesus.

Today's Challenge: Consider ways that your life can more closely imitate the life of Jesus.

Aug 1

"Near Running Water"
by Jimmy Mack

He is like a tree planted near running water, that yields its fruit in due season, and whose leaves never fade. ~ **Ps 1:3**

Prayer life gives us courage to live out the gifts and fruits of the Holy Spirit. LIFE Runners capture this essence knowing that our faith walk, like our running life, will hit many walls; at the 20-mile mark, the 20-month mark in our faith life, or even the 20-second mark in our prayer life. We are faithful and run as a prayer to defend children in the womb. We plant seeds by our charity to provide support for mothers and fathers tempted to abort their child, and offer healing support for post-abortion women, men, and families.

Today's Challenge: Every time we show God's love to abortion-vulnerable and post-abortion parents, we plant and water with confidence, knowing that God will help them grow.

"Do Not Fear"
by Bernadette Costello

Aug 2

Even the hairs of your head have all been counted. Do not be afraid. You are worth more than many sparrows.
~ Lk 12:7

The enemy uses fear to distract and cripple us, but God gives us a spirit of power and self-control. He loves us perfectly just how we are. He provides us everything that we need so there is never a reason to worry. Abortion-vulnerable parents are paralyzed by fear. Pray for them to hear His voice and feel His embracing love through you.

Today's Challenge: Sing to God in thanksgiving when you do not have answers because you can count on Him to take care of everything.

Aug 3

"In God We Trust"
by Dr. Rich Reich

Now as for you, you have so many good things stored up for many years, rest, eat, drink, be merry! ~ Lk 12:19

Jesus called the rich man a fool for preparing his own future. In our independent culture, most people would prefer to rely on their own provisions than to depend on what God promises to provide. Jesus teaches us to pray for only what we need today. We are fools when we trust in years of financial security instead of trusting in God. He has promised to supply all that we need.

Today's Challenge: Help abortion-vulnerable women trust that God will provide for their needs and the needs of their unborn child.

"Be Kind"
by Amy Kosta

Aug 4

Be kind to one another, compassionate, forgiving one another as God has forgiven you in Christ. ~ Eph 4:32

We so often hear abortion termed as the "war on women" or "murder", which is true, however we must approach this subject with a loving and forgiving heart, just as Jesus would have done. We must not let our frustrations lead us to anger and hatred, which are the tools of Satan. It is wise to use our frustrations to become more firmly convicted in our quest to protect the unborn. The use of negative words and accusatory comments will only build walls in communication. Let us go forth armed with love, compassion and forgiveness to fight the battle.

Today's Challenge: Share your love with others by extending a warm smile and a friendly greeting to all those whom you pass today.

Aug 5

"Time is Short"
by Lisa Skowron

What I mean, brothers, is that the time is short. For this world in its present form is passing away. ~ 1 Cor 7:29,31

Paul urges the Corinthians to be diligent and decisive about keeping centered on the gospel and advancing the kingdom of God, rather than focusing their attention on present circumstances. Paul says that even our marriages, times of grieving, pursuing the pleasures of life, and rejoicing when we are happy, though they are all good things when put in the right perspective, are less significant relative to the priority of God's kingdom and His purposes. They are temporal and we are better off focusing on the eternal. Pray for God to reveal anything in your life that might be taking your focus and attention away from doing what God wants.

Today's Challenge: Are you being diligent and proactive in defending life, or are you sitting complacent and disengaged while watching those around you being led by the Holy Spirit?

"The Power of Love"

by Fr. Jonathan St. Andre

Aug 6

Love is patient, love is kind. It is not jealous, love is not pompous, it is not inflated, it is not rude, it does not seek its own interests, it is not quick-tempered, it does not brood over injury, it not does not rejoice over wrongdoing but rejoices with the truth. ~ 1 Cor 13:4-6

Saint Paul reminds us that the greatest of all gifts is love! When we receive this greatest spiritual gift of love from the One who is love, we can bear every circumstance and still move forward, believe in goodness even when darkness seems to overwhelm, hope in what is unseen, and endure to the end. What a gift that we can incarnate the love of Jesus Christ in small and great ways.

Today's Challenge: Spend a few moments using the passage above as an examination of how you are loving. You can do this by inserting your name in every place where it says the word "love" and consider how you could be more loving for abortion-vulnerable parents.

Aug 7

"Just Breathe"
by Bernadette Costello

Perish the day on which I was born, the night when they said, 'The child is a boy!' ~ Job 3:3

Job cried out for God to end his life and questioned why he was even born. There may be times that we feel that hopeless, but God never abandons us. Abortion-vulnerable parents appear to be screaming on the inside as though no one can hear their agonizing cries. They clearly experience Job's pain. It looks as though they are gasping for even one breath of fresh air. When we speak with authentic love to them, they suddenly begin to breathe, as though for the first time. It is a visible sign of the Holy Spirit working through us for them.

Today's Challenge: Pray for those who work tirelessly to help abortion-vulnerable parents choose life for their unborn children.

"Dry Bones"
by Joshua Bachman

Aug 8

Then He said to me, prophesize over these bones, and say to them, dry bones, hear the word of the Lord! ~ Ez 37:4

God could will any result He wants, but He chooses to invite us to participate in His works. It is another blessing that is beyond our comprehension; His ways are not our ways. Glorify Him and participate in His will for creation. Take action to protect mothers and the unborn. Promoting the dignity of human life is part of God's plan for His creation, and what an honor it is to be given the opportunity to be God's servants.

Today's Challenge: Take a moment before each action to thank God for allowing you to be part of His works.

Aug 9

"Be Not Afraid"
by Tess Allman

At once Jesus spoke to them, 'Take courage, it is I; do not be afraid.' ~ Mt 14:27

God is our stronghold, our deliverer, and protector. There is nothing that we should fear. We must cling to Jesus' words. A loving Catholic father at my parish offered to adopt any baby in danger of being aborted. That opened my eyes to see what it means to be not afraid. For all of us, this pro-life courage will manifest itself in different ways. God bless us all with courage and help those who have lost their way.

Today's Challenge: Let us pray to discern how we can be more courageous in our efforts for the unborn. Let us pray for those who believe in the sanctity of life but who are still afraid to speak up.

"Consecrate"
by Pastor Rick Foreman

Aug 10

Consecrate yourselves for tomorrow, God will do great things among you. ~ Jos 3:5

The word consecrate is a verb requiring action and in the connotation of this scripture, serves as a foundational structure of faith that God is going to do great things. The scripture really represents the particular purpose of LIFE Runners, who witness and pray to end abortion. We can rest assured that God is going to do great things among us in preserving life and ending abortion. The Lord's purpose is always to give life. Many plans are in a man's mind, but it is the Lord's purpose for him that will stand. We know this world will pass away, but His word will endure forever.

Today's Challenge: Have confidence that He will indeed bring victories through your faith.

Aug 11

"Renew me Lord"
by Bernadette Costello

A clean heart create for me, God; renew within me a steadfast spirit. ~ Ps 51:12

We often harden our hearts to protect ourselves from being hurt, but the reality is that our spirit can only be lifted high on eagle's wings if we keep loving and allowing others to love us. Any good in us is from Him who loves us perfectly. Our desire to be renewed is a gift from God. Sing praise to God that He chooses you to stand up for the sanctity of life. He chooses you to be His hands and feet.

Today's Challenge: Pray for God to renew your spirit, so it is within His heart that you live, move, and have your being.

"Time Wasted"
by Bernadette Costello

Aug 12

Thus says the Lord, 'I have heard your prayer; I have seen your tears. Now I will add fifteen years to your life.'
~ Is 38:5

The world as we know it is passing away, but be encouraged because whoever does the will of God lives forever. Many years in this world goes by in just a blink of an eye. We do not know the year, date, or time that we will be called home. Offer every prayer, work, joy, and suffering to Him daily. He calls us to love our neighbor, feed and clothe the poor, visit the sick and imprisoned, and share His love and mercy with others.

Today's Challenge: Waste time with Jesus, discern where God is calling you to serve the least of these, the precious most innocent unborn, and then act.

Aug 13

"One of a Kind"
by Whitney Compton

Before I formed you in the womb I knew you, before you were born I dedicated you, a prophet to the nations I appointed you. ~ Jer 1:5

Wow! He knows us inside and out, our hearts, thoughts, abilities, and needs. He will help guide us to accomplish that which He dedicated us to do. We need to remind others to use the gifts that God gave them. Like us, the unborn have unique gifts and talents intended to be used for God's glory. If we invite the Lord into our lives daily, our unique gifts – along with His grace – will bring His light to the world.

Today's Challenge: Pray for the mother who feels alone today; pray that the Lord sends her someone to remind her that she and the child in her womb are unique.

"Fountain of Life"
by Lauren Muzyka

Aug 14

With You is the fountain of life, O Lord. ~ Ps 36:9

Scripture provides a total blueprint for how we should live our lives - physically, emotionally and spiritually. These guidelines provide the prescription to live a healthy, happy and whole life. We are admonished to put the Lord first above all things, to love our neighbor as He loves us, and to treat our bodies as a temple of the Holy Spirit. How can we serve God's kingdom to the best of our ability if we do not follow His instructions for an abundant life?

Today's Challenge: In your prayer time today, ask yourself the following questions. Do I put God first above all things? Am I taking care of myself and others? Now, ask God to give you the grace to make any needed changes.

Aug 15

"Disordered Desires"
by Dr. Rich Reich

Again, the kingdom of Heaven is like a merchant's search for fine pearls. When he found one really valuable pearl, he went back and put up for sale all that he had and bought it. ~ Mt 13:45-46

Jesus taught us in the Our Father not only how to pray, but also how to desire. He taught us that the priority of our desires should be in the same order as our petitions in the Our Father. Our first desire should be for our Father's name to be hallowed. Then for God's kingdom to come. The culture of death promotes a selfish and disordered desire. They believe that a person is responsible for their own happiness and objectify others as a means for achieving this happiness.

Today's Challenge: In order to defeat the culture of death, we need to keep our desires in order by placing God first and His kingdom before all else.

"Position of Humility"
by Dr. Rich Reich

Aug 16

I served the Lord with all humility ~ Act 20:19

Although Jesus was in the form of God, He did not count equality with God a thing to be grasped. Instead, He took the form of a servant, being born in the likeness of men. And being found in human form, He humbled Himself by becoming obedient to the point of death, even death on a cross. As Christians, we have a responsibility to be humble, obedient servants like Christ. In our Pro-Life apostolate, may we continue to be humble servants no matter our position.

Today's Challenge: May we never view ourselves greater than another, and may our hearts reflect the humility of Christ.

Aug 17 — "Be Useful Salt"
by Dr. Rich Reich

You are the salt of the earth. But if salt loses its taste, with what can it be seasoned? It is no longer good for anything but to be thrown out and trampled underfoot.
~ Mt 5:13

In ancient warfare, the victors would trample salt underfoot into the croplands of the defeated nation making the soil infertile and ensuring the vanquished people would not return to vitality and military strength. Satan aims to do that by keeping us spiritually barren, thus preventing us from bearing God's fruit. However, Jesus saves us. He turns us into "the salt of the earth" so that we may preserve and add flavor to the world. We are the salt of the earth with the responsibility to share with others the bitterness of abortion.

Today's Challenge: Be useful salt and become active in your local LIFE Runners chapter. These chapters require leadership, assistance, spiritual guidance, and active participation in Pro-Life events; otherwise, these chapters may risk becoming tasteless and flat.

"Conquer Evil with Good"
by Dr. Rich Reich

Aug 18

But I say to you, offer no resistance to one who is evil.
~ Mt 5:39

Jesus tells us to offer no resistance to one who is evil, but that does not mean that we are not supposed to resist Satan. Rather it means that we are not to struggle against flesh and blood but against the spiritual forces of evil. In defense of the unborn, we are passionate about what we believe and that can sometimes lead to anger; however, we are asked not to take revenge. We must look at Jesus as our model. Jesus' lack of resistance at Calvary brought down the kingdom of darkness and humanity was saved.

Today's Challenge: Conquer evil with good. Show love towards those who do not share our same value for the dignity of all human life. Lead them to Jesus!

Aug 19 — "Rewards in Heaven"
by Kevin McNicholas

Take care not to perform righteous deeds in order that people may see them; otherwise, you will have no recompense from your heavenly Father. ~ Mt 6:1

Jesus talked about demonstrating humility in our giving. I have known fantastically generous people who have given so much in the service of others but have expected to be acknowledged and celebrated. Jesus tells us that the good that we do without others' knowledge will be rewarded in Heaven. More specifically, the good that we do for God, rather than for human praise or attention. If we receive an earthly reward, our grace is diminished in Heaven. If we do good in God's service for Him and Him alone, He will richly bless us. This is the reward worth waiting for, to hear at the end of our lives "well done, My good and faithful servant!"

Today's Challenge: Serve abortion-vulnerable parents for God, who is love.

"Wolves in Sheep's Clothing"
by Alice Chapman

Aug 20

Beware of false prophets, who come to you in sheep's clothing, but underneath are ravenous wolves. By their fruits you will know them. ~ Mt 7:15-16

Planned Parenthood advertises that they help women decide among their options when faced with an unplanned pregnancy. They present themselves as a professional, caring organization whose staff are available to answer questions and help women find the services they need. They warn visitors on their website to avoid pregnancy help centers because they are "fake clinics" who attempt to scare them into not having abortions. This is the ultimate irony because it is exactly the tactic they use to encourage women to abort. They are a modern-day wolf in sheep's clothing. Lest we get discouraged, God reminds us that every tree that does not bear good fruit will be cut down and thrown into the fire.

Today's Challenge: Support your local pregnancy help center with your time and treasure to reach those who need help the most.

Aug 21

"Obey God"
by Kevin McNicholas

But Peter and the apostles said in reply, 'We must obey God rather than men.' ~ Act 5:29

By refusing the temptations of society and choosing to obey Him, we will be counter-cultural, we will be different, and we will be despised in the world's eyes. These are all good things! Jesus never said that we were going to have an easy stroll through life by following Him. The result, eternity in Heaven, is worth far more than fleeting pleasures here on earth. What the world and popular culture have to offer is not true joy and will not lead us to eternal life with Christ.

Today's Challenge: Pray that we always remain courageous in defending life from conception to natural death, no matter the difficulty.

"Persecution"
by Scott Casmer

Aug 22

When they heard this, they were infuriated, and they ground their teeth at him. ~ Act 7:54

Stephen called out society about their evil ways that were in opposition to God's law. Society was not willing to accept the word of God and change their ways. They cried out in a loud voice, covered their ears, and rushed upon him together. They threw him out of the city and began to stone him. When the issue is as grave and divisive as abortion, the resistance to the message and the associated persecution today is comparable. Regardless of the suffering we encounter, we need to continue to love those who oppose us. Stephen gave us an outstanding model for this when he prayed right before his death, "Lord, do not hold this sin against them."

Today's Challenge: Pray for the grace to be able to lovingly communicate the way your faith has led you to an unwavering Pro-Life position.

Aug 23

"Eternal Life"
by Dr. Rich Reich

I give them eternal life, and they shall never perish.
~ Jn 10:28

Jesus promised to give us eternal life; a life lived in Heaven forever with Him. We receive this gift of eternal life when we are baptized. Many people seek to accept this gift but do not seek to give their lives to Jesus now. This is perplexing. Eternal life is not just a happy, everlasting life, but a life of total love for Jesus. Why would someone seek to be with Jesus forever in Heaven if they do not desire a relationship with Him now? This lack of commitment to the Christian ideals of eternal life are paralleled with the inactive Pro-Lifer. Why would someone call themselves Pro-Life if they are not willing to actively defend the unborn and the dignity of all human life?

Today's Challenge: If you are Pro-Life, give your time, talent, and treasure to Pro-Life ministries to help put an end to abortion.

"Obedience is Love"
by Dr. Rich Reich

Aug 24

Whoever has My commandments and observes them is the one who loves Me. And whoever loves Me will be loved by My Father, and I will love him and reveal Myself to him." ~ Jn 14:21

Obedience is one of the ways that we express our love to God. Sin and death entered the world through disobedience, but salvation entered the world through Jesus' obedience. The Holy Spirit will always give our conscience a nudge when we are struggling with disobedience. Pray for the grace to hear His voice. We must strive to die to ourselves and our selfishness. Dying to self and acting in obedience to Him is one way of showing our true love and commitment to God.

Today's Challenge: Be an example to others through your obedience to Christ. Show them that abortion is wrong.

Aug 25

"True Joy"
by Whitney Compton

I have told you this so that My joy might be in you and your joy might be complete. ~ Jn 15:11

The Lord created us by love, for love, and to be in union with Him in love. Love is a motivator, and the fullness of love is joy. In everything we do and in each soul we spiritually adopt, especially the souls of the unborn; it is essential to be rooted in Jesus. We can look to Jesus as a true example of this authentic joy. He suffered out of love for us so that we might be joyfully redeemed.

Today's Challenge: Go out with joy and bring others, with love, into the joy of Jesus.

"Love Those Who Condemn"
by Scott Casmer

Aug 26

And they said, 'Believe in the Lord Jesus and you and your household will be saved.' ~ Act 16:31

Silas was with Paul, who invoked the name of Jesus to exorcise a spirit from a slave who was being unjustly used by her owners for profit. The public condemned them and had them jailed. Upon suddenly being freed, Paul and Silas did not seek revenge on the jailor, but instead shared their faith and baptized his whole family. This passage has multiple analogies to those engaged in the Pro-Life movement today. Many are condemned for showing others Jesus' love for all human life.

Today's Challenge: Identify people close to you who do not understand the sanctity of life. Pray for their conversion and for an opportunity to discuss life issues with them.

Aug 27 — "I Am With You Always"
by Paul Westendorf

Go, therefore, and make disciples of all nations. And behold, I am with you always, until the end of the age.
~ Mt 28:19-20

These verses have been labeled the "Great Commission". It is Jesus' final instruction to His church. Today we live in a world that continues to promote the importance of worldly things, supports putting emphasis on one's own wants and satisfaction regardless of others, enacts laws that are contradictory to God's teachings, and impedes Christian organizations with government interference. Times have not really changed and Jesus' commission for us surely has not changed. We are called to be witnesses for Christ, to spread His word, and to show His love to all. Do not fear the persecution, rejection, and hardships because He is with us always.

Today's Challenge: God gave us a spirit of power, love, and self-discipline. Be courageous and persevere in the battle to end abortion.

"America, Defend Life!"
by Dr. Patrick Castle

Aug 28

Do not be afraid. Go on speaking, and do not be silent, for I am with you. ~ Acts 18:9-10

God speaks these words to all LIFE Runners, encouraging us forward to speak up for the unborn. We shall not fear because God is with us. St. John Paul II exhorts, "If you want equal justice for all, and true freedom and lasting peace, then, America, defend life!" Defending God's gift of life is precisely what motivated me to serve in the Air Force and lead a Pro-Life apostolate. We are all called to remain on active duty with God. Our Pro-Life mission demands we move forward, forward, always forward!

Today's Challenge: Strive to publicly wear your LIFE Runners "REMEMBER The Unborn" jersey at least once every week - to help change hearts and minds for saving lives.

Aug 29 — "Choose Life"
by Fr. Joseph Oganda

The Lord redeems the lives of His servants; no one incurs guilt who takes refuge in Him. ~ **Ps 34:22**

God has set before us life and prosperity, death and doom. Loving God and choosing to run in His path with the speed of love and charity, at a pace of prayer and conversion of heart makes us true LIFE Runners. Refusing to listen to the word of life is death to one's soul. Rejecting to put into practice the wisdom of salvation is a cause of doom to one's heart. When disciplining the desires of our flesh, let us first drink from a common cup of love.

Today's Challenge: Offer your running and walking as a prayer to end abortion and let every step bring you closer to our Lord, Jesus Christ.

"Diffusion"
by Dr. Rich Reich

Aug 30

Mary took a liter of costly perfumed oil and anointed the feet of Jesus and dried them with her hair; the house was filled with the fragrance of the oil. ~ Jn 12:3

You probably know through experience that one squirt from a perfume bottle can quickly fill a room with fragrance. In a parallel passage to this reading in Mark's gospel, the text reveals that Mary broke the jar of expensive perfume just before she used it to anoint Jesus. Can you imagine the diffusion going on in that house spreading the beautiful fragrance of flowers? Reflect on the diffusion of LIFE Runners as we spread the beautiful Pro-Life message and pray for the unborn.

Today's Challenge: Be an active part of spreading the Pro-Life message to others.

Aug 31

"Face The Cross"
by Shane Kapler

Will you lay down your life for Me? ~ Jn 13:38

Jesus posed that question to Peter after the great apostle rashly declared his ability to follow the Master anywhere, even if this meant forfeiting his own life. Each of us presumes far too much on our ability to face the cross. We forget that we are continually in need of a fresh infusion of God's grace to accept our share of Christ's cross. Unless we are living in contact with the Master, continually offering ourselves to Him, and asking Him to give us His strength, we will fall when threatened by the world.

Today's Challenge: Pray the Chaplet of Divine Mercy. Call out to God for His mercy on this wayward world. Petition Him, through the passion of His only begotten Son, to convert nations that do not value life.

"Visible Faith"

by Kevin McNicholas

Sep 1

She said to them, 'They have taken my Lord, and I don't know where they laid Him.' ~ Jn 20:13

Mary Magdalene speaks what is perhaps one of the most important lines of faith in this verse. She accepted and proclaimed that Jesus is Lord, the Son of God, and who did she say this to? The risen Christ Himself! She had a past life that was considered unforgivable in society at that time, but Jesus only saw the person that God created. We may feel that our sins and the sin of abortion are ones that cannot be forgiven but that is never the case with Christ. He loves us perfectly just how we are, and He can redeem anyone!

Today's Challenge: Pray for the gift of faith. Belief is an acceptance of a truth, whereas faith is a choice to live that belief.

Sep 2 — "Do We Recognize Him?"
by Dr. Kevin Vost

Look at My hands and My feet, that it is I Myself... touch Me and see, because a ghost does not have flesh and bones as you can see I have. ~ Lk 24:39

Jesus appeared to His apostles after His resurrection, but they did not recognize Him at first. After bidding them peace, Jesus asked why they were troubled and asked them to look at Him, at His hands and feet. Do we recognize Him in every mother's womb? Do we have to see through an ultrasound image the tiny hands and feet to know that the child nestled within is an image of God?

Today's Challenge: In what areas of life do you not recognize Christ? Do you see Him in the unborn? Recommit yourself today to seeing Christ in people and places where our culture does not.

"Reborn and Unborn"
by Dr. Rich Reich

Sep 3

Nicodemus said to Him, 'How can a man once grown old be born again?' ~ Jn 3:4

Jesus replies to Nicodemus' question of being reborn with the response that one must be born from above in order to see the kingdom of God. Only those who are reborn have their sins forgiven and have a relationship with God. The freedom of choice that God grants us is not the freedom to take innocent life, but to choose who will be our Lord... Jesus or Satan. For those who know God, this is not a moral dilemma. God is clear in His message when He said, "I call Heaven and earth to record this day against you, that I have set before you life and death, blessing and cursing. Therefore, choose life, that both you and your seed may live."

Today's Challenge: Pray that our culture of death will be reborn and see that the gift of life outweighs the choice of death.

Sep 4

"Good News"
by Fr. Daren Zehnle

Go and take your place in the temple area, and tell the people everything about this life. ~ Acts 5:20

The angel of the Lord told the apostles to go back into the public square and proclaim without fear the truth of the passion, death, and resurrection of our Lord Jesus Christ. We are all called to share the good news. Those who are considering aborting their child and those who have already done so need to hear the joy of the gospel in our words and see it in our lives. Be bold, be a disciple, put on the armor of Christ and go forth to all nations proclaiming the good news!

Today's Challenge: Let us seek out one person to whom we can bring the joy of the gospel to give them hope amid strife.

"Prophetic Witness"
by Shane Kapler

Sep 5

... turn our mourning into gladness and our sorrows into wholeness. ~ Es 12:23

Faced with the extermination of her people, Queen Esther was seized with mortal anguish. Esther went to the Lord on behalf of her people and asked Him to give her prophetic words that would influence the king. She understood that God was the true sovereign, to whom all those in power must answer, and so she lay prostrate upon the ground, together with her handmaids, from morning until evening, begging the Lord to intervene. When thinking of the threat faced by our unborn brothers and sisters, we share Esther's anguish. We likewise need to embrace Esther's battle plan to fall on our faces before the Lord, asking Him to give us prophetic words.

Today's Challenge: Ask the Lord to pour out the grace of conversion upon all government officials who can impede and reverse abortion policies.

Sep 6 — "Seeds of Plenty"
by Dr. Rich Reich

For the measure with which you measure will in return be measured out to you. ~ Lk 6:38

Most people in the time of Jesus worked as farmers. The landowner would pour as much seed into the fold of the worker's garments as they could hold. The worker would then carry the seeds to the field and sow them by hand until the fold of their garments were empty. Then they would return to the seed-pile for more seeds and the process was repeated until all fields were sown. Jesus tells us that those who give themselves to Him will be given much. When we serve Jesus through our Pro-Life apostolate, He will multiply our resources and sow our "REMEMBER The Unborn" message to save lives.

Today's Challenge: Return to the seed-pile by recruiting new LIFE Runners to spread the Pro-Life message.

"Trust & Hope"
by Ed Heigl

Sep 7

Cursed is the man who trusts in human beings, who seeks his strength in flesh, whose heart turns away from the Lord. Blessed is the man who trusts in the Lord, whose hope is the Lord. ~ Jer 17:5,7

Jesus tells us that blessed are they that place their hope and trust in God. With faith, we can be made pure, clean and whole in this life and in our eternal life that is to come. Those who decide to lock their hearts from the inside turn away from God. They become part of the greatest tragedy of human existence, which is the failure to become a saint and the loss of Heaven. We must always stand up for the gift of life. Pray for every soul to recognize God's presence in all human life, born and unborn.

Today's Challenge: Allow God to bring good out of all suffering in our lives as we strive to remain faithful to His will.

Sep 8

"Obey to the Letter"
by Dr. Rich Reich

Amen, I say to you, until Heaven and earth pass away, not the smallest letter or the smallest part of a letter will pass from the law, until all things have taken place. ~ Mt 5:18

Jesus challenges us to follow God's law to the letter as He did, and not allow it to be twisted to our own liking. We imitate Jesus in the desert when we pray, fast, and engage in acts of spiritual self-discipline to overcome Satan's temptations. The culture of death tempts us to justify the killing of innocent unborn children. We must ask the Holy Spirit to guide us to the truth where culture influences our morals.

Today's Challenge: Where have we compared ourselves with others rather than to God's standards? Align yourself with God's standards and obey as Jesus obeyed.

"Answering The King"
by Dr. John Sturm

Sep 9

Whoever is not with Me is against Me. ~ Lk 11:23

Jesus' stern love cut very deeply to flush out the Pharisees' evil intentions in front of the crowd that was still marveling at the miracle of Jesus casting out the demon. In our struggles to promote life it seems that every argument in support of the dignity of life is countered with a deception that either denies life really exists or rationalizes why one's need outweighs the life of another. However, if we are running for life on God's team, there is no room for second guessing His commandments to respect life without exception.

Today's Challenge: Imagine yourself in the crowd with Jesus being wrongly accused of sorcery. Would we speak out on Jesus' behalf and risk our reputation? Pray that we might always speak out to expel abortion from our culture.

Sep 10

"A Father's Loss"
by Shane Kapler

My son, my son Absalom! If only I had died instead of you! ~ 2 Sam 18:33

David's kingdom was in rebellion; and, like any king, he wanted it to end. However, the rebellion was led by his son Absalom. Battle ensued and David's kingdom was preserved but at the loss of his son. It was a victory that crushed David's soul. There are many in today's world whose success has come at the cost of their child, through abortion. They suffer knowing that they ended their child's life to ensure their own misguided sense of survival. Their suffering often leads them to wishing they could now exchange places with their child.

Today's Challenge: Jesus does not want anyone to succumb to despair. Whether you personally know someone in this position or not, call out to God to pour His merciful forgiveness into their lives.

"Abusive Power"
by Bishop Joseph Coffey

Sep 11

The girl hurried back to the king's presence and made her request, 'I want you to give me at once on a platter the head of John the Baptist.' ~ Mk 6:25

Most of us know the details of the death of John the Baptist. Herod shamefully honored his pledge to the daughter of Herodias who wanted John's head on a platter. As king, Herod had power over life and death. He abused that power. John was an innocent man. Justice Byron White in his dissent of Roe v. Wade called the decision an exercise in "raw judicial power." In an abortion, the powerful unjustly condemn the weak and most vulnerable among us. We will never stop fighting this gross injustice. St. John the Baptist, pray for us.

Today's Challenge: Pray for those in authority that they use their power to protect all of the innocent unborn children.

Sep 12 — "Temple of the Holy Spirit"
by Kevin McNicholas

May your eyes watch night and day over this temple, the place where You have decreed You shall be honored.
~ 1 Ki 8:29

King Solomon prayed a very prophetic prayer here, as Jesus made reference several times in the gospels to His own body as a temple that would be destroyed and raised up in three days. God decrees that He shall be honored in each of our bodies, most importantly in our spirit, as our faith drives everything we do. We are commanded to glorify God with our body. Take special care of it spiritually, physically, and mentally.

Today's Challenge: Abortion damages one temple and destroys another, bringing dishonor to God. Pray for every soul to recognize our bodies as a gift to house the Holy Spirit.

"Well-formed Conscience"
by Joshua Bachman

Sep 13

When Solomon was old his wives had turned his heart to strange gods, and his heart was not entirely with the Lord.
~ 1 Ki 11:4

Solomon's affections for those who did not uphold God's law deformed his conscience. As a result, he turned his heart to strange gods. Who or what do we allow to influence our conscience most strongly? Subtle influences may not immediately turn us away from remembering the unborn, but they can color our conscience gradually. Perhaps we may find ourselves hesitant to offer life-saving information because of who is present. Or maybe we find it harder to disagree when abortion is offered as the best solution to a crisis pregnancy. Seek God and be wary of affections and influences that could gradually undermine a well-formed conscience.

Today's Challenge: Properly form your conscience by reading the word of God and spending time in prayer daily.

Sep 14

"Listen to God"
by Diane Overmann

I am the Lord, your God. Hear My voice. ~ **Ps 81:8,10**

How often do we escape our noise-polluted world to spend time in silence with God? Just as we hunger for others to listen to us, God craves our attention to listen to Him. He lovingly asks us to be quiet, so He can whisper His affections. God invites us to personal communication with Him. Sometimes I choose to listen and shine His light. I think of all the aborted children that were denied the right to choose God and shine His light. Who has the right to deny another the right to life? God is whispering the answer to the world.

Today's Challenge: Try to spend at least a few minutes in silence daily, inviting God to gently whisper to you. Listen and respond.

"Living Faith"

by Pastor Matthew Lim

Sep 15

What good is it, my brothers and sisters, if someone says he has faith but does not have works? Faith of itself, if it does not have works, is dead. ~ Jam 2:14,17

James argues that true faith is a living faith from God that transforms a person inside and out. True faith in Jesus Christ will always be seen in how one relates to others in the world. What a grand reminder that every effort to defend the unborn, as with all works of righteousness, transcends mere political or social issues. Let us not labor only for the physical rescue of the helpless but also for their spiritual redemption through the gospel of Jesus Christ.

Today's Challenge: In the light of God's word, take some time today for a personal faith examination.

Sep 16

"Let God Steer"
by Kevin McNicholas

You have no idea what your life will be like tomorrow. ~ Jam 4:14

We never have any idea what God may have planned for us, but faith tells us that His ways are better than ours. He has a greater plan than we could ever imagine. We are naturally inclined to try to control what goes on around us. As Christians, we are humbled and subject to aligning our lives in accordance with God's will. This reminds me of a tandem bicycle analogy. You sit on the back seat and pedal, and God sits on the front seat and steers… don't try to take God's seat! So today, pedal even harder to help end abortion soonest.

Today's Challenge: Share this great news of God's plans being better than we could even imagine with someone tempted to abort their child.

"You Belong & Are Loved"
by Jean Noon

Sep 17

Salt is good; but if the salt has lost its saltiness, how will you season it? ~ Mk 9:50

Jesus came to save every soul, to bring the good news that each one belongs and is loved unconditionally by God. The message that grace reconciles and restores is not yet central to our culture. This grace is offered not in spite of our imperfection but because of it. Pro-Life ministry brings God's spirit of pro-love to every encounter from womb to tomb. As this message becomes our culture's message, hearts change, just as God intends.

Today's Challenge: Are you willing to cooperate with grace so that God's spirit can renew the face of the earth?

Sep 18 — "Blessed Perseverance"
by Mike Sanders

You have heard of Job's perseverance and have seen what the Lord finally brought about. The Lord is full of compassion and mercy. ~ Jam 5:11

How many times do we reflect on the past and complain or look to the future and get anxious or depressed? I began to be afraid when I was diagnosed with stage IV cancer, but I quickly learned that God truly is full of compassion. I thought that my life was ending quickly in this world, but the Lord answered many prayers. He held me in His arms during my time of suffering just as He has held me and protected me in all things from birth to now, and just as He is doing with you. Pray that you do not grumble or complain so that you may be blessed as you persevere in your struggles.

Today's Challenge: Persevere in the fight to end abortion and trust that God will always protect you.

"Make Straight the Way"
by Dr. Patrick Castle

Sep 19

I am the voice of one crying out in the desert, 'Make straight the way of the Lord!' ~ Jn 1:23

John the Baptist was an army of one crying out in the desert. We are still in the desert crying out for an end to abortion, but we are not alone! We have the armor of God to stand against the ploys of the devil. We also have the communion of saints and His body, the Church. In Jesus' name, we are stronger than the power of satan and his spawns. Jesus said that we will do greater things in His name than He did. Be confident as you clear the path for Him to lead our world out of darkness.

Today's Challenge: Take time to learn about the spiritual weapons that God provides, so you are prepared for every battle.

Sep 20

"Stop!"
by Dr. Rich Reich

Samuel said to Saul: 'Stop! Let me tell you what the Lord said to me last night.' ~ 1 Sam 15:16

The Lord spoke to Saul through Samuel, telling him to stop disobeying Him. Without Samuel speaking out, Saul would have continued thinking that he was obeying the Lord. Samuel's presence was critical in delivering God's message to Saul. Sometimes we listen to others more than we listen to the Lord. Your peaceful prayers outside the abortion facility may speak louder than you imagine. Your presence communicates to the abortion-vulnerable parents, the escorts, the employees, and the cars driving by that what is happening inside the abortion facility is not pleasing to God.

Today's Challenge: Allow the Lord to speak through you to those considering abortion.

"Mustard Seeds of Faith"
by Paul Nurse

Sep 21

It is like a mustard seed that, when it is sown in the ground, is the smallest of all the seeds on the earth. But once it is sown, it springs up and becomes the largest of plants.
~ Mk 4:31-32

We look forward in peace and assurance as we strive to build the kingdom of God. We remember Christ's promise that whatever we ask in His name, He will do, so that the Father may be glorified in the Son. We ask the Lord this day, as a community of believers trusting fully in His power, to sow the culture of life fully into our world. We thank the Lord for all the mustard seeds that He has sown in our lives.

Today's Challenge: Continue to persevere in faith and know we are truly a global team, united in prayer, building the culture of life from all the corners of the earth!

Sep 22

"God's House"
by Shane Kapler

This I seek, to dwell in the house of the Lord. ~ Ps 27:4

The house of the Lord... the Temple planned by David, built by Solomon, rebuilt by Zerubbabel and Joshua, rededicated by Judas Maccabeus, and enlarged by Herod. Under the Old Covenant it was God's house, Heaven's embassy on earth. Under the New Covenant, however, we discover the realities to which the Temple pointed; Jesus, His Church, and the fullness of life in Christ that the church will enjoy in Heaven! To dwell in these New Covenant realities requires intentionality on our part; in the words of the psalm, we seek. And we do this most successfully in prayer, where we ask.

Today's Challenge: Take advantage of His nearness by visiting a church or adoration chapel where He dwells under the appearance of bread. While in His presence, ask for His power to save our unborn brothers and sisters.

"Lost & Found"
by Lauren Muzyka

Sep 23

What man among you having a hundred sheep and losing one of them would not leave the ninety-nine in the desert and go after the lost one until he finds it? ~ Lk 15:4

It is so tempting to detest the abortion facility worker who convinces abortion-vulnerable parents that abortion is their only option. The Lord tells us in scripture that it is not the will of our Father that one of these little ones should perish. God wills and wants all His children to come back to Him with contrite hearts. We must remember that all of us fall short of the glory of God, and none of us have clean hands. Let us take the victory that God has in our lives and be His hands and feet. May we reach out to abortion facility workers, knowing that He wills for them to be saved too.

Today's Challenge: Pray for all those in the abortion industry, that they may come to Christ and know His saving love.

Sep 24

"Divine Intimacy"
by Dr. Rich Reich

Because into a soul that plots evil, wisdom does not enter, nor does she dwell in a body under debt of sin. ~ Wis 1:4

God's eternal plan of love is to espouse us to Himself forever. He wants us to live in Him and have an intimacy with Him that is beyond anything we could ever imagine. The love shared between a married man and woman is only a hint of the mystical eternal union that God desires with us. However, God who is absent of sin cannot be near us when we are in a sinful state. If we wish to be close to God, we must repent of our sins. Our desire for communion with Him can be confused with our selfish desires. We all share in the internal craving for unity with God.

Today's Challenge: Pray for abortion-vulnerable parents and for the healing of post-abortion families.

"Gratitude for Life"
by Fr. Vince Bertrand

Sep 25

We always give thanks to God, the Father of our Lord Jesus Christ, when we pray for you, for we have heard of your faith in Christ Jesus and the love that you have for all the holy ones. ~ Col 1:3-4

We remain strong in our faith and keep a joyful heart by practicing the virtue of gratitude every day. We also help those around us come to a deeper awareness and appreciation for the gift of life. May we never forget to thank God each morning for the wonderful gift of a new day and conclude each day by thanking God for all His blessings. LIFE Runners, your love for Christ and for life, your courage and enthusiasm, your prayer and support for one another, is truly an inspiration.

Today's Challenge: Pray the Respect Life rosary, as we work to bring a greater respect for life from conception to natural death in our local communities, our nation, and our world.

"Equipped for the Journey"
Sep 26
by Alice Chapman

He sent them out to proclaim the Kingdom of God and to heal. He said to them, 'take nothing for your journey, no staff, nor bag, nor bread, nor money - not even an extra tunic.' ~ Lk 9:2-3

Journeys during that time were accomplished primarily on foot through desolate areas where wild animals and thieves preyed upon vulnerable travelers. We know the disciples bravely set out, proclaiming the gospel, and successfully carried out the mission to which Jesus appointed them. God always equips His followers for the tasks He calls them to. Go out and respond lovingly to our lost brothers and sisters who sadly support abortion.

Today's Challenge: Commit to wearing your "REMEMBER The Unborn" jersey in public often to impact hearts and minds.

"Pro-Life Solidarity"
by Dr. Rich Reich

Sep 27

Jesus said to him, 'Do not prevent him, for whoever is not against you is for you.' ~ Lk 9:50

We compare ourselves with others to see who is greatest, yet we are all members of the same body of Christ. If one member suffers, all the members suffer; if one member is honored, all the members share joy. We are called to give encouragement and love to one another. We need to stand, walk, and run together in Pro-Life solidarity. Take no more pride in the good that God says and does through you, than in that which He says and does through someone else.

Today's Challenge: Research Pro-Life ministries in your area and help support them with your time, talents, and treasure.

Sep 28 — "There's only One God"
by Barb Honeycutt

All this you were allowed to see that you might know the Lord is God and there is no other. ~ Dt 4:35

Moses tells us that there is only one God. We cannot have two masters; either we are with Him or against Him. Being lukewarm is unacceptable. Our society conditions us to believe that joy can be obtained without God. Unfortunately, many succumb to the lie that possessions and self-dependence will fulfill what their hearts desire. Those choices lead to emptiness, every single time. Abortion is a selfish choice that only leads to darkness and despair. We must teach others what Christ teaches us; to deny ourselves, take up our cross and follow Him.

Today's Challenge: Pay close attention to the ways God is trying to get your attention each day. Respond faithfully.

"Standards"
by Dr. Rich Reich

Sep 29

They sacrificed to demons their own sons and daughters.
~ Ps 106:37

Science is a systematic enterprise that builds and organizes knowledge about our world. It does this through measurements that are made based on standards. God set our standards for living way before our existence, and He has imprinted His standards on the hearts and conscience of every human being. Our secular culture has not maintained the integrity of these moral standards and has allowed them to corrode. Even the simplest standard to remember, "thou shall not kill", continues to deteriorate.

Today's Challenge: Do not allow today's secular culture to corrode the moral standards God has imprinted in your heart. Maintain the truth that all life is sacred, born and unborn.

Sep 30

"Gehenna"
by Dr. Rich Reich

Woe to you, scribes and Pharisees, you hypocrites. You traverse sea and land to make one convert, and when that happens you make him a child of Gehenna twice as much as yourselves. ~ Mt 23:15

Jesus was speaking to the scribes and Pharisees, but He could equally state today, "Woe to you, pro-abortion people. You traverse to your nearest inner-city abortion facility to make one pro-choice convert, and when that happens you make them a child of Gehenna twice as much as yourselves." Jesus was speaking about the satanic child-sacrifice under some of the godless kings of Israel at that time. Today, abortion facilities are slaughtering unborn children, and our society is normalizing it.

Today's Challenge: Pray for abortion-vulnerable parents who are feeling pressured by their so-called loved ones to abort their child.

"God's Mercy and Goodness"
by Matthew Laugeman

Oct 1

You have searched me and you know me. ~ Ps 139:1

The sadness we feel for our brothers and sisters who walk in darkness is real. The disappointment and anger we feel as our soldiers battle ever-increasing darkness in our world is deep. But St. Paul teaches us to conduct ourselves as worthy of God who calls us into His kingdom. Let us remember how blessed we are to be called. Let us persevere and be strengthened by the spirit of compassion. Allow Jesus' words in Matthew's gospel to ignite a fire within you against worldly hypocrisy.

Today's Challenge: Let your light shine in every dark corner. All In Christ for Pro-Life!

"Power of Intercession"
Oct 2
by Dr. Rich Reich

While the two men walked on farther toward Sodom, the Lord remained standing before Abraham. ~ **Gen 18:22**

The Lord allowed Abraham to intercede for the cities of Sodom and Gomorrah instead of punishing them for their grave sins. We should never underestimate the power of intercession. Many people pray at abortion facilities all over the country to prevent women from committing the grave sin of abortion. We are intercessors asking God to save the unborn and the abortion-vulnerable parents from the suffering of abortion. Countless testimonies have been recorded about lives being saved at abortion facilities due to the presence of people praying.

Today's Challenge: Take every opportunity to pray for an end to abortion.

"Bridges"
by Mike Sanders

Oct 3

From Heaven the Lord looks down and sees all mankind; from His dwelling place He watches all who live on earth, He who forms the hearts of all, who considers everything they do. ~ Ps 33:13-15

I've run over many bridges in my lifetime. One bridge I recently crossed was during the LIFE Runners A-Cross America Relay. Not even a half-mile into my run a massive dog came barreling at me. You know how the Lord sends relief but because of our pride and stubbornness, we do not recognize it? That is what happened with me. God sent 3 vehicles past me, but I just stood there frozen and afraid. When I realized my reaction of fear, I prayed for one more to come by and sure enough it did. God sent me this person to cross over an area of fear. God provides everything that we need. Share this truth with abortion-vulnerable parents who are afraid.

Today's Challenge: As we cross over our bridges of life, may we hope for the Lord and trust in His holy name.

Oct 4

"Serpents and Doves"
by Scofield Thomas

Behold, I am sending you like sheep in the midst of wolves; so be shrewd as serpents and simple as doves. ~ Mt 10:16

"Beware of people, for they will hand you over to courts and scourge you in their synagogues, and you will be led before governors and kings for My sake as a witness before them and the pagans." It is easy to see this happening in our daily lives. The sanctity of life is not valued by our society. As our freedoms, rights and values are increasingly constricted it seems as if the encroaching darkness we feel is the slow fading of hope. However, God is our eternal light and refuge!

Today's Challenge: Allow God to shape your environment to convey the simple message that all life is a gift from God.

"Oh, My Soul"
by Stephen Holinaty

Oct 5

Bless the Lord, O my soul; and all my being, bless His holy name. Bless the Lord, O my soul, and forget not all His benefits. ~ Ps 103:1-2

When people see the destruction and tragedy of a hurricane, they react and most people want to help. Yet abortion occurs daily but most of society does nothing to help. I wonder if people saw the destruction of abortion if they would react and want to help. After they see what happens to the child, the physical and emotional scars on the woman, and the crude conditions in abortion facilities… would they react and want to help?

Today's Challenge: For those who argue against life, remind them that Jesus said, "Let the little children come to Me, and do not hinder them, for the kingdom of Heaven belongs to such as these."

Oct 6 — "Burial Places"
by Dr. Rich Reich

Were there no burial places in Egypt that you had to bring us out here to die in the desert? ~ **Ex 14:11**

Moses led the Israelites into the desert rescuing them from slavery in Egypt; however, the Israelites were not grateful and responded that they would have rather died as slaves in Egypt. They did not trust Moses or have faith that God would provide for them in the desert. Many abortion-vulnerable parents find themselves in the same state of desperation as the Israelites. They do not have faith that others will be there to help support them and their child. We need to support women and help protect them from choosing the womb as a burial place for the unborn.

Today's Challenge: Check out the websites of your local Pro-Life apostolates and pray about how the Lord might use you to help their efforts.

"Faithful Sowing"

by Pastor Ron Burtz

Oct 7

Still other seed fell on good soil, where it produced a crop, a hundred, sixty or thirty times what was sown. ~ Mt 13:8

Unlike other parables, Jesus took time to explain this one to His disciples saying that the seed represents the gospel of the kingdom, and that the different soils represent different individuals and the condition of their hearts. Jesus tells us to keep proclaiming the gospel, trusting God to ready the soil of people's hearts to receive it. The same is true with our Pro-Life message, we will not always encounter open hearts and minds as we call our culture to choose life. We will face outright hostility and rejection. It is our duty to keep sowing the seeds and trusting God to bring about the harvest in His time.

Today's Challenge: Are you faithfully sowing the seeds of the gospel of life? Pray for His grace to listen and respond boldly.

Oct 8

"Service of Life"
by Dr. Kevin Vost

The Son of Man did not come to be served but to serve and to give His life as a ransom for many. ~ Mt 20:28

When the mother of James and John asked that Jesus sit them at His left and right sides in His kingdom, He told her that she did not know what she was asking. He gathered all the apostles together and said, "whoever wishes to be great among you shall be your servant; whoever wishes to be first among you shall be your slave." Rulers of earthly kingdoms make their authority felt in many ways. Today, rulers use their authority to ensure that human lives may be lawfully crushed even before they are born. Christ suffered on the cross to defeat sin and death, making everlasting life possible for us.

Today's Challenge: Are you willing to bear afflictions and persecutions by defending and serving the least and the weakest among us?

"Seeds of Truth"
by Jenn Garza

Oct 9

The evil one comes and snatches away what has been sown in his heart. ~ Mt 13:19

Society fails to recognize human life in its purest and most innocent form. This comes from a simple yet profound ignorance of God's desire for us to commit our lives to building His kingdom. The culture has sucked up the life-giving water and made dry the path upon which we try to sow the seeds of truth - hardening it and making it impossible for the roots of reality to take hold. Without first cultivating the soil of our lost brothers' & sisters' hearts, we cannot expect to see the fruits of the seeds we sow.

Today's Challenge: Let us make fertile the ground upon which we run, so that the seeds of truth we spread along the way may become tall trees of truth and produce a bountiful harvest.

Oct 10

"Pray and Obey"
by Stacey Wollman

But when you pray, go into your room, close the door and pray to your Father, who is unseen. Then your Father, who sees what is done in secret, will reward you. ~ Mt 6:6

Pray, Pray, Pray and Obey, Obey, Obey. This is the simple formula for a Christ-follower! This passage of scripture simply lays out how we are to pray. The Lord's prayer is strategic. It demonstrates that we are to honor God. We ask Him to bring His will to earth as it is in Heaven, declaring our trust in Him for our livelihood each day through provision. With continued humility through acknowledging sin in our lives, we surrender our right to be offended at others who have sinned against us. We ask for His protections and deliverance regarding the schemes of the devil who tries to attack, distract and bring evil into our lives. Prayer is the key to ending abortion.

Today's Challenge: Our prayers are heard by our living God. Do not make prayer a monologue, make it a conversation.

"Of Most Value"
by Shane Kapler

If your eye is sound, your whole body will be filled with light; but if your eye is bad, your whole body will be in darkness. ~ Mt 6:22-23

What do we value most in life? It is important because it shapes how we view the world. It is critical that we place value on our relationship with Christ. We must evaluate our actions and stances based upon whether they bring us closer to, or farther away from, God. A true Christian understands that the killing of children within the womb is abhorrent to God and will not make peace in any way, shape, or form. Our society refuses to admit what it values most because it is not God - love, generosity, and sacrifice. No, it is pleasure, economic stability, and security - none of which are bad in themselves, but evil when put above God and His will.

Today's Challenge: Ask the Holy Spirit to fill your heart with knowledge, wisdom, and understanding.

Oct 12

"Womb or Tomb"
by Dr. Rich Reich

For now the Lord has spoken who formed me as His servant from the womb. ~ Is 49:5

The Church celebrates the Feast of the Holy Innocents which proclaims the significance of life in the womb. In our abortion-minded and contraceptive culture of death, we need constant reminders of God's great plans for all life, including life before birth. The culture of death proclaims that the womb is a tomb. The culture of life emphasizes the womb is a place for God to anoint His children. Those like Mary, who had a crisis pregnancy and chose life, are blessed by God. God intended the womb to be a life-giving place.

Today's Challenge: Jesus welcomed children. Let us do the same.

"The Author of Life"
by John Audino

Oct 13

It is He who gives to everyone life and breath and everything. ~ Acts 17:25

What a powerful truth! Life, the world, and all of creation would not exist without God. This truth must be the driving force of Pro-Life ministry. To deny another person their right to life is to rebel against the author of life Himself. The fact that God is the source of our life gives each person infinite value. Those who fight for the least among us are true disciples of the risen Lord. May the author of life bless the work of those whose lives are founded upon the truth that "it is He who gives to everyone life and breath and everything."

Today's Challenge: Make an act of faith by renewing your commitment to fight, sacrifice, and pray for the safety of each irreplaceable life that is threatened by abortion.

Oct 14

"Pain to Joy"
by Shane Kapler

You will weep and mourn while the world rejoices.
~ Jn 16:20

Jesus spoke those words to prepare the apostles for His crucifixion. He continued by promising, "you will grieve, but your grief will become joy. When a woman has given birth to a child, she no longer remembers the pain because of her joy." We grieve the loss of our unborn brothers and sisters and our witness to life is met with the world's derision. But Jesus will bring the atrocity of abortion to an end. We will rejoice as mothers trade the pain of abortion for the joy of holding their newborn children.

Today's Challenge: Petition our Lord for the repose of our aborted brothers' and sisters' souls, and their parents' healing.

"To Serve"

by Pastor Matthew Lim

Oct 15

For the Son of Man did not come to be served but to serve and to give His life as a ransom for many. ~ Mk 10:45

Jesus' selfless life fulfilled the requirements of God's Law, making His death a perfect sacrifice on man's behalf. Combating for the unborn is a vital act of serving on behalf of the helpless, and true serving in Christ extends to the unworthy and even to those who will respond with rejection. God's grace is not reserved for only the lovable and the deserving. Through us, God's freely given grace extends to all.

Today's Challenge: While endeavoring to serve the unborn, strive to be a genuine servant for those who do not share our views on the sanctity of life. Such a testimony of God's grace may be the only gospel they hear.

Oct 16

"Road to Emmaus"
by Dr. John Sturm

Were not our hearts burning within us while He was speaking on the road and explaining to us the scriptures? ~ Lk 24:32

Jesus was a stranger the apostles encountered on the road to Emmaus, but He touched their hearts through the words of scripture. As we run and walk with our "REMEMBER The Unborn" jersey, it is easy to read the reactions of people we encounter. Some are encouraged and supportive, and some shout disapproval or turn away. Therefore, our running becomes a pilgrimage of sacrifice and a prayer to end abortion. Every run is an opportunity to evangelize and serve.

Today's Challenge: Be able to explain the science that proves each of us is a distinct and complete human being from the moment of conception.

"Grace"

by Shane Kapler

Oct 17

They laid hands on Peter and John and put them in custody until the next day. ~ Acts 4:3

Many in Pro-Life ministry have shared Peter and John's experience of being taken into police custody because of their witness to Jesus and His teachings. We need to ask God, every single day, for the grace to pay whatever price is asked of us. Grace changed Peter from a man too frightened to acknowledge Jesus into a mighty shepherd who was crucified rather than cease proclaiming Jesus' power to heal and save. Defend the unborn against abortion even if others persecute you, calumniate you, set traps for you, take you to court or kill you. No child should be deprived of the right to be born.

Today's Challenge: Pray at a nearby abortion facility.

"Love and Humility"
Oct 18
by Dr. Rich Reich

Mary said, 'Behold, I am the handmaid of the Lord. May it be done to me according to Your word.' ~ Lk 1:38

Why would the Creator of the entire universe humble Himself in becoming a creature? It is because God is love, and the root of love is humility. With more experience of true love we will grow in humility. Mary clearly knew true love as she responded humbly, "I am the handmaid of the Lord. May it be done to me according to your word." Mary is a model for all human beings. Like her, we should see ourselves as servants of the Lord and ask for the grace to live fully for Him.

Today's Challenge: Pray that every woman who finds herself pregnant follows Mary's example of love and humility by choosing to say yes to life.

"Faith Opportunities"

by Shane Kapler

Oct 19

Jesus said this to test him because He Himself knew what He was going to do. ~ Jn 6:6

Jesus used the sight of the crowd as an opportunity to draw out an expression of Philip's faith, and He uses a variety of bold circumstances in our lives to do the same thing. Philip was surprised by the predicament they found themselves in, but Jesus already knew how He was going to respond. Philip missed his opportunity to respond in faith when Jesus asked him how the crowd would be fed. We all miss opportunities to respond in faith. We should ask the Lord daily to lead us in everything that we do.

Today's Challenge: Next time the culture of death tempts you to despair, place your faith in God. Pray immediately, Lord, I'm completely devastated by this; but You saw this moment long before I was born, and You know what I need to move forward. Please show me what I need to do. Please give me the grace.

Oct 20

"Face of an Angel"
by Dr. Rich Reich

All those who sat in the Sanhedrin looked intently at him and saw that his face was like the face of an angel.
~ Acts 6:15

An international all-star team of debaters challenged St. Stephen, "but they could not withstand the wisdom and the Spirit with which he spoke." They presented him before the Sanhedrin speaking falsely against him, but all the Sanhedrin could see was the face of an angel. The same can be seen at abortion facilities around the world. Most Pro-Life people gather to pray and advocate peacefully. However, some do not handle their righteous anger well and are not effective in helping others choose life. Like the Sanhedrin, even those who do not know the truth of abortion can recognize the face of an angel.

Today's Challenge: Do not let your anger against abortion destroy your message of God's mercy and love.

"Jesus Hears"
by Laurie Edwards

Oct 21

Like a sheep He was led to the slaughter, and as a lamb before its shearer is silent, so He opened not his mouth.
~ Acts 8:32

While praying at the fifth Station of the Cross, my eyes fell upon Jesus' ear. The truth echoing in that moment was that Jesus, so silent in His passion as described by the prophet Isaiah, hears the silent cries of the unborn on their way to the slaughter. His tender heart carries within it the cries of the hurting, the lonely, and the innocent.

Today's Challenge: Build upon whatever understanding someone has about who God is, what that says about who we are, and what that means about how we treat one another - including those in the womb.

Oct 22

"Sight in Light"
by Dr. Kevin Vost

Immediately things like scales fell from his eyes and he regained his sight. ~ Acts 9:18

Sometimes it takes a dramatic, traumatic event to get us to see things in a new light and to start doing things right. That is a lesson St. Paul learned so very well on his road to Damascus. The horrific event at the 2013 Boston marathon finish line provided us with the sight of countless spontaneous acts of courage and compassion. It inspired us to value life more deeply in every possible way. Every precious child or adult who lost life or limb started life in their mother's womb. Let's pray to God that scales will fall from all of our eyes, and we will fully cherish every life from the moment of conception to natural death.

Today's Challenge: Pray to receive St. Paul's missionary zeal in helping our culture see the truth of abortion.

"Humble Healing"
by Dr. Rich Reich

Oct 23

But his servants came up and reasoned with him, "My father, if the prophet told you to do something extraordinary, would you not do it? All the more since he told you, 'Wash and be clean'?" ~ 2 Kgs 5:13

Naaman, the army commander of the king of Aram, was seeking to be cured of his leprosy; however, he suffered from a condition far worse... his own pride. Once he swallowed his pride, he was healed. Many women and men feel embarrassed and afraid to let others know that they have an unplanned pregnancy, so they seek abortion. Some carry the suffering of abortion for the rest of their lives without ever being healed because of their shame and pride. When we humble ourselves, we open the door to God and to healing, for the Lord "is stern with the arrogant but to the humble He shows kindness."

Today's Challenge: Seek to continue the mission of the servants of Naaman by guiding others to the channels of God's grace by which they can be healed.

Oct 24

"Stirred Up"
by Dr. Rich Reich

The Lord heard her prayer. As she was being led to execution, God stirred up the Holy Spirit of a young boy named Daniel, and he cried aloud, 'I am innocent of this woman's blood.' ~ **Dn 13:44-46**

The corrupt law was going to execute an innocent life until the Holy Spirit stirred up a young boy named Daniel to take action. Without Daniel speaking out against the unjust law, the innocent life would have been put to death. Daniel heard the Holy Spirit stirring in his heart and heeded God's command, "Rescue those who are unjustly sentenced to death; don't stand back and let them die."

Today's Challenge: We are called to speak out against the unjust law that legalizes the killing of innocent unborn children. Pray for an end to abortion now and pray at your local abortion facility as often as possible.

"Standing Firm"

by Shane Kapler

Oct 25

You need endurance to do the will of God and receive what He has promised. ~ Heb 10:36

We must stand firm and continue to confess the truth despite opposition and persecution. The dignity of life, the beauty of the family, and the right to life from conception to natural death are all essential aspects of this truth. "Our present sufferings are not worth comparing with the glory that will be revealed to us." To persevere we must be people of prayer, doing everything we can to allow Christ's grace to flow through us unhindered. Jesus warns us, "because of the increase of wickedness, the love of most will grow cold, but the one who stands firm to the end will be saved."

Today's Challenge: This kind of perseverance is supernatural. It comes from the hand of God. He wants to give it to you, but He will not force it upon you. Ask Him for this grace daily.

Oct 26

"Vote Pro-Life"
by Dr. Patrick Castle

Fathers, bring them up with the training and instruction of the Lord. ~ Eph 6:4

God commands fathers to bring up, not abort, their children. He directs fathers to teach their children His ways. Our Founding Fathers embraced this responsibility. In 1782, Congress printed the Bible for the common good of schools and the inhabitants of the United States. Out of the 56 founding fathers who signed the Declaration of Independence, 29 of them had seminary or Bible school degrees. Thomas Jefferson said, "The care of human life and happiness, and not their destruction, is the first and only legitimate object of good government."

Today's Challenge: Help save the unborn and their families from destruction by taking a stand with your prayers, words, and votes for Pro-Life!

"Vote for Christ"
by Dr. Patrick Castle

Oct 27

Take care to guard against all greed, for though one may be rich, one's life does not consist of possessions.
~ **Lk 12:15**

Let's not let fear about the economy cause us to compromise the Pro-Life issue which trumps all other voting issues. Without life, the other issues are meaningless. The fear and pain surrounding abortion is a web of evil that often muffles people from supporting life, even in the safety of a faith community. Boldly act to keep the Pro-Life issue in the spotlight during elections. It is not too late to be God's instrument in changing and encouraging hearts to speak up. Whenever you need motivation to defend life, close your eyes and remember the thousands of innocent babies dying every day. Remember our innocent Christ dying on the cross so that all can live.

Today's Challenge: Spend one hour with Christ praying in front of an abortion facility this weekend.

Oct 28

"Change"
by Bishop Thomas Paprocki

Let what you heard from the beginning remain in you.
~ 1 Jn 2:24

We cannot tolerate abortion. It must end now, and to end it, we must change. The kind of change we need to end these atrocities is to put into practice what we have heard from the beginning about God's commandments. Therein, however, lies one of our nation's greatest challenges. With the teaching of religion banned from public schools and with so many parents who do not teach children about God, where do children learn about God's commandments? Teach people to love one another, to cultivate peace, and to live with good will rather than mere tolerance.

Today's Challenge: It is no wonder that Saint John Paul II prophetically called ours a culture of death. We must change. Promote a culture of life and peace.

"Spiritual Deadness"
by Dr. Kevin Vost

Oct 29

Let the dead bury their dead. But you, go and proclaim the kingdom of God. ~ Lk 9:60

This striking play on words implies "let the spiritually dead bury the physical dead; mine is a message of life." Today we see the spiritual deadness that leads millions to the burial, no, to the disposal of, not the bodies of their parents, but of their unborn children. Many fail to see that God's message honors all life and promises eternal life. "No one who sets a hand to the plow and looks to what was left behind is fit for the kingdom of God."

Today's Challenge: Let us then dedicate ourselves fully to Christ's message of respect for all human life. Let it show through us so that whether we are praying, running, evangelizing, counseling, or voting, we will proclaim the kingdom of God and His message of life.

Oct 30

"Not Debatable"
by Dr. Patrick Castle

The harvest is abundant, but the laborers are few.
~ Lk 10:2

We are the few laborers, and the harvest is abundant. We have labored in planting seeds of truth, God caused the growth, and now it is harvest time. We harvest the fruits of the Spirit: love, joy, peace, forbearance, kindness, goodness, faithfulness, gentleness and self-control. When we face a culture that debates the sanctity of life, these fruits keep us strong to hold the line and vote Pro-Life because the sanctity of life is not debatable.

Today's Challenge: "Think and pray very carefully about your vote because a vote for a candidate who promotes actions or behaviors that are intrinsically evil and gravely sinful makes you morally complicit and places the eternal salvation of your own soul in serious jeopardy."

"You Knit Me"
by Gov. Kristi Noem

Oct 31

For You created my innermost being; You knit me together in my mother's womb. I praise You because I am fearfully and wonderfully made; Your works are wonderful. ~ Ps 139:13-14

Since the day that abortion was legalized, millions of babies in America have been murdered - their potential ripped away, their laughter silenced before it had a chance to start. Every life, starting from the time of conception, has dignity and value. As believers, we know that value not only comes from the existence of life, but from the very fabric of our being. Scripture states that we are made in the very image of our Creator - we are the product of His hands. He created our innermost being. It is His breath in our lungs.

Today's Challenge: Pray prophetically over the future of our nation. Pray that eyes will be opened to the evil of abortion. Pray that the Lord would place people in power who are able to confront this injustice and defend unborn lives.

Nov 1

"God Prunes"
by Ed Heigl

He takes away every branch in me that does not bear fruit, and everyone that does He prunes so that it bears more fruit. ~ Jn 15:2

The lives of the Saints give us great examples of imperfect individuals who were open to God's will in their lives and who allowed Him to prune their lives. Pruning involves real sacrifice of our will and even suffering. From this pruning by God, they bore much fruit and became models of how we should live our lives. We must be steadfast in our faith to always bear witness to life as a God given gift. Wearing the LIFE Runners jersey is a very powerful witness that impacts souls by this very simple but courageous act.

Today's Challenge: Read Psalm 122 and then pray for all of those involved in the business of abortion.

"Holy Sacrifice"
by Fr. Joseph Totton

Nov 2

For by one offering He has made perfect forever those who are being consecrated. ~ Heb 10:14

I was challenged by a couple friends to start running. Since I was not inclined to do so, they appealed to my strong Pro-Life sentiments. Suddenly, a task which felt impossible and was uninteresting became a holy sacrifice which also changed my understanding of my role in the Pro-Life ministry. Whatever sufferings we endure in His name can contribute to the redemption of the world. They can be offered to atone for the many sins committed against God's love, including those sins which repudiate the sanctity of life. I may run a mile or from "sea to shining sea," but the Lord will take each step, those of pain and those of glory, and unite them to His saving sacrifice.

Today's Challenge: Do not limit the spread of God's word or the action of His grace in your life by the perceived limits of your capabilities. Give the Lord everything and allow Him to show you the abundance of His divine generosity!

Nov 3

"The Song of Life"
by Fr. Joseph Oganda

For at the moment the sound of your greeting reached my ears, the infant in my womb leaped for joy. ~ Lk 1:44

Elizabeth is our model of hope, and Mary is our model of faith. The dark cloud of sin may be blocking our vision and preventing us from seeing the victory of the light, the power of life over death, the gift of God's love for all humanity, a savior who is named Jesus. God, our light, has illuminated our path, "Fear not, do not be discouraged for the Lord is in your midst and will renew you in love." God has chosen us as a people of His own heart, a people of His own inheritance, and He is our shield against the disdain for life. Nothing is impossible for God; life will always prevail, for it is beautiful.

Today's Challenge: With joy and gladness, we join our voices with Mary in a song of, "Yes, Lord, let Your will be done to us."

"Emancipation Proclamation"
by Dr. Patrick Castle

Nov 4

See what love the Father has bestowed on us that we may be called the children of God. ~ 1 Jn 3:1

The blood of abortion has flooded our country since January 22, 1973. Pro-Lifers have spent years in the desert. One moment with abortion is too long. We have spent too much time and energy blaming the pro-abortion side. Let us change our focus from them to us. We can do much more to ensure another generation does not have to suffer the reality of abortion. In 1863, President Lincoln issued the Emancipation Proclamation that freed God's children who were enslaved in America. "Nobody should have the freedom to choose to do what's morally wrong."

Today's Challenge: Let us put our Pro-Life faith in action to make an Emancipation Proclamation for all of God's children, born and unborn.

Nov 5

"Holy Light"
by Pastor Don Bird

The Spirit of the Lord is upon me because He has anointed me to bring glad tidings to the poor. He has sent me to proclaim liberty to captives and recovery of sight to the blind, to let the oppressed go free, and to proclaim a year acceptable to the Lord. ~ Lk 4:18-19

Jesus is standing before his hometown friends and is invited to read the words from the prophet Isaiah, just as many had done before Him. Jesus said, "Today this scripture is fulfilled in your hearing." Jesus was proclaiming to those who would hear that He knew why He was sent by His heavenly Father. Every person is created for a special purpose. My heart aches for the unborn who will not survive to fulfill their purpose. God desires to shed light on the atrocities of abortion, to proclaim to the world the worth of every human life, born and unborn, and to bring recovery of sight to those who are blind to the evils that so easily lurk amongst us and within us.

Today's Challenge: Proclaim to the world that every life has a purpose that must not be silenced but freed to live into the fullness of God's calling.

"Authentic Freedom"
by Dr. Rich Reich

Nov 6

For freedom Christ set us free; so stand firm and do not submit again to the yoke of slavery. ~ Gal 5:1

Our hedonistic society views liberation as the freedom to indulge one's desires without restraint; however, this does not promote genuine freedom. This promotes bondage to one's cravings. It is God's will that we should be sanctified by learning to control our bodies in a way that is holy and honorable, not like the heathen, who do not know God. Abortion is the deliberate disregard for the sanctified life God intends for us. Do not be a slave, instead open your hearts to the Lord's gift of redemption.

Today's Challenge: Break free from the restraints of selfish desire and seek the authentic freedom that Christ offers.

"Lighten the Load"

Nov 7

by Dr. Cliff Ozmun

Woe also to you scholars of the law! You impose on people burdens hard to carry, but you yourselves do not lift one finger to touch them. ~ Lk 11:46

In contrast to Jesus' two commands to love God and love our neighbors, the Pharisees imposed 613 laws, which they proceeded to circumvent regarding themselves. These laws placed unbearable burdens on adherents. Our Father expects not empty tithes of bitter herbs, but righteous sacrifice that frees the oppressed, feeds the hungry, shelters the poor, clothes the naked, and cares for family. Every day many women find themselves facing the challenge of unplanned pregnancy. Factors such as social stigma, scarce resources, and lack of support from families are all heavy burdens weighing on mothers considering abortion. As Christians, we ought to help lift these burdens and lighten their loads.

Today's Challenge: Contact your local pregnancy resource center today. Pray, donate, serve. Enlist others to do the same.

"His Words"
by Kathryn Lopez

Nov 8

The Lord is faithful in all His words. ~ Ps 145:13

When we surrender our lives to God, we are united to the most powerful love, the strength that no evil can suppress or conquer. Without knowing the love of a merciful God, we are limited, our impact is finite, we keep ourselves from our fullest, deepest potential and from living the will of the Father. Meditating on the empty tomb, we remember. Gazing at Jesus' presence in all the tabernacles of the world, we are drawn deeper. It is in the daily care and feeding of our souls that we can live the gospel truth. Let others not only know we are Christians by our love but be unmistakably drawn to the source of our hope, joy and strength.

Today's Challenge: Be a light to the world, proclaiming truth in the simplest but also the bravest of ways. Defend life from conception to natural death.

Nov 9

"Planted in Humility"
by Dr. Patrick Castle

I planted, Apollos watered, but God caused the growth.
~ 1 Cor 3:6

If we are not grounded in humility, we are no good to ourselves, others or God. How very humbling that our Creator calls us to be His co-workers in building His kingdom here and now. We have planted and watered, but God has caused our growth. I recently saw parts of a documentary about three young men who fasted from all food for seven continuous days. I was taken by the humility of the cameraman who also fasted but was never seen or heard from during the documentary. May we humbly encourage parents tempted to abort their child to choose life, and offer healing support for post-abortion women, men, and families.

Today's Challenge: Humbly join our Pro-Life action team, LIFE Runners, as a runner or walker.

"Expose Sin"
by Dr. Rich Reich

Nov 10

Looking around at them all, He then said to him, 'Stretch out your hand.' He did so and his hand was restored.
~ Lk 6:10

Jesus asks the man with the withered hand to display his weakness to him before a crowded synagogue. The man obeys Jesus and his hand is restored. The man was probably deeply embarrassed about his disability. He found the courage and humility to expose his weakness, and he was healed. St. Faustina once said, "A soul does not benefit from the Sacrament of Confession if it is not humble. Pride keeps it in darkness. The soul neither knows how, nor is it willing, to probe with precision the depths of its own misery. It puts on a mask and avoids everything that might bring it recovery." Lord, give me the courage and humility to remove my mask and expose my sins to You, that I may be restored.

Today's Challenge: Pray for post-abortion parents to have the humility and courage to expose their sins to the Lord so that He may heal them.

Nov 11

"Conquer Pride"
by Paige Castle

Be joyful in hope, patient in affliction, faithful in prayer.
~ **Rom 12:12**

There is a deep sense of pride and separation in the Pro-Life ministry at times. Faith, humility, patience, and joy conquer pride, and are essential to Pro-Life ministry. We must strive to be the Pro-Lifer that Mary is, deep in courageous love and humility. We cannot fight the prideful holocaust of children with prideful lack of teamwork. St. Padre Pio said this about the Blessed Virgin Mary, "Some people are so foolish that they think they can go through life without the help of the Blessed Mother. Love the Madonna and pray the Rosary, for her Rosary is the weapon against the evils of the world today. All graces given by God pass through the Blessed Mother."

Today's Challenge: Pray to God for an increase in humility and love and ask the Blessed Virgin Mary for guidance daily.

"Forgiveness"
by Doug Wollman

Nov 12

Jesus said to the woman, 'Your faith has saved you; go in peace.' ~ Lk 7:50

Post-abortion women often feel an unbearable amount of shame and regret. Abortion leaves in its destructive path nothing but fatal consequences to the unborn child and life-long torment to families. Although sin and destruction have sought to creep in and impose even more death, separation, and pain by the choices made, there is forgiveness through Jesus Christ who removes sin. Jesus abounds in His ability to reach even the deepest penetrating scars. The forgiveness of Jesus provides freedom from years of torment, guilt and shame.

Today's Challenge: Pray for post-abortion women, men, and families to be vulnerable to Christ who will heal them.

Nov 13

"Appointed Time"
by Steve Castle

There is an appointed time for everything, and a time for everything under the heavens. ~ Ecc 3:1

It seems like we have lost sight of the fact that God is in control. We are consumed with planning every detail of our life, yet scripture tells us that God has appointed every moment of our life. He knew us before we were knit in our mother's womb. He counted the number of hairs on our head. He knew where we would sit and where we would stand. He is with us at every moment of joy and pain, when we laugh and when we cry, and when we dance and when we mourn. We are told that there is a time to be silent and a time to speak. Be a voice for those without a voice - the unborn.

Today's Challenge: Speak boldly in the world wherever God has planted you.

"Divine Mercy"

by Dr. Gregory Thompson

Nov 14

If you forgive others their transgressions, your heavenly Father will forgive you. ~ Mt 6:14

Jesus, being God, humbled Himself to bear our sins. He was spat on, mocked, beaten beyond recognition, tortured severely, and nailed to a cross to die for you and me. Then said, "Father, forgive them, they know not what they do." He did this while we sinners said, "crucify Him", and helped hammer nails into His hands and feet. He gives us infinite Divine Mercy for all our sins, how can we not forgive offenses that are minute in comparison to all the ways we crucify Him and are forgiven? Jesus, give us the grace to have an attitude of love for those who threaten to destroy life and possibly their own souls. Holy Spirit, speak through me so they accept the grace from You to turn away from abortion, and run to You.

Today's Challenge: Do whatever you can to receive the body, blood, soul and divinity of Jesus every day, and if not possible try to engage in Adoration daily. Then ask Jesus to use you to bring souls to Him. There is nothing more important.

Nov 15

"Just Follow"
by Jack Spring

It is He who gives to everyone life and breath and everything. ~ Acts 17:25

It is by the very breath of life in all of those around us, the born and the unborn, that we see God and are prompted to seek after Him. He is our everything. And so, like St. Brendan the Navigator of ancient Ireland who sailed for seven years in search of The Land of Promise, we are sailors on a high sea, sometimes with neither rudder nor sail, uncertain of our way. We take encouragement from each other, and then are called to trust that God will be our wind and compass. And then, even on the darkest night, when it seems we're hopelessly lost, we gaze upward to see that God has fixed the stars in the heavens to lead us home, if we'll just follow.

Today's Challenge: Be the change in the world you seek. Trust God to show you the way.

"Path to Life"

by Dr. Patrick Castle

Nov 16

You will show me the path to life. ~ Ps 16:11

A colleague shared her experience at Planned Parenthood when her daughter scheduled an abortion. A couple weeks before the scheduled abortion, the daughter asked her Mom if she would ever have an abortion, the Mom said no. The Mom drove her daughter to the scheduled abortion. She was surprised that she was not allowed to accompany her daughter during "the procedure." After waiting for about an hour, the Mom went out to her car to escape the dark and cold environment. After not being allowed to see the ultrasound, the daughter decided not to abort her child. Her Dad had paid for the abortion, and he was upset his daughter did not go through with it. What was your path to life?

Today's Challenge: How much do you love your family, friends, and neighbors? Courageously show them the path to life.

Nov 17

"Godly Perspective"
by Fr. Justin Damien Dean

Teacher, we want You to do for us whatever we ask of You. ~ Mk 10:35

James and John are driven to achieve their goal of egocentric self-exaltation, without considering the collateral damage. That is the scenario when a new life intrudes into the myopic world of self-absorbed persons. If new life will cause inconvenience or embarrassment, that life is expendable. Though we may have the right perspective on the issue of the sanctity and inviolability of human life from the moment of conception, we must all be aware of the possibility of losing a Godly perspective in other areas of our lives.

Today's Challenge: Ask God to rouse our collective conscience in relation to life issues and our individual consciences in the area of our personal blind spots.

"Serving Others"
by Kristina Hernandez

Nov 18

So when He had washed their feet and put His garments back on and reclined at table again, He said to them, "Do you realize what I have done for you?" ~ Jn 13:12

Jesus knew that He would suffer the pain of betrayal, be scourged, and be crucified. Knowing all of this, He still chose to wash the feet of His disciples. The Master kneeling in front of the slave, setting a beautiful example of how we are to imitate Him. The enormous love Jesus has for us is astounding, and He calls us to follow Him. Do we love our enemies and pray for those who are misguided, especially those who work in abortion facilities? Our dignity as humans comes from having been made in the image and likeness of God – each one of us. Every person you meet has this dignity. How will you imitate Christ and serve someone today?

Today's Challenge: Watch the movie The Passion of the Christ and recall what Christ did for you on the cross.

Nov 19

"Lies for Sale"
by Dr. Rich Reich

They assembled with the elders and took counsel; then they gave a large sum of money to the soldiers, telling them, "You are to say, 'His disciples came by night and stole Him while we were asleep.'" ~ Mt 28:12-13

This was Satan's first attempt to keep the great news of Jesus' resurrection from a world enslaved by death. Today, money from large organizations is funding the culture of death. Planned Parenthood spends millions of dollars each year to ensure that taxpayers will continue subsidizing its abortion services. They generate so much by making false claims about how public funding reduces the number of abortions, but the numbers tell a different story. The abortion industry is all about making money and not at all about protecting the lives of women and their unborn children. What is your price? Can you be bought? If so, satan will buy you like the guards who pocketed the money and lied about Jesus' resurrection.

Today's Challenge: Do not let greed prevent you from being a witness to the Lord. Serve the Lord and not money.

"Jesus Meets Us"
by Teresa Laugeman

Nov 20

And it happened that while they were conversing and debating, Jesus drew Himself near and walked with them. But their eyes were prevented from recognizing Him.
~ Lk 24:15-16

There are moments daily that most of us do not notice or give any attention to Jesus' presence in our lives. The two disciples left Jerusalem, most likely feeling exhausted, confused, lost, and overwhelmed, much like a young mother must feel when she finds herself pregnant and not knowing where to turn. The gospel shows us that Jesus meets us exactly where we are in our journey, no matter how broken, unworthy, and overwhelmed we may feel. He is there for us whether we recognize Him or not. It is by being the example of Jesus' love that eyes will be opened, and He will be recognized as the giver of all life.

Today's Challenge: Meet others where they are on their journey and share the good news of Jesus' redeeming love.

"Transformation"

Nov 21

by Kevin Lowry

Then the two recounted what had taken place on the way and how He was made known to them in the breaking of the bread. ~ Lk 24:35

Sometimes the presence of Jesus isn't immediately obvious. Just like the two disciples on the road to Emmaus, we can be downcast as we reflect on circumstances of life. Yet as we recognize the Lord, our perspectives are transformed. When a child is conceived, his or her presence may not be immediately obvious either. Yet this child will transform the parents - and others - in beautiful ways. Jesus' mother Mary modeled faith in all circumstances when she responded yes. Look at the transformation of humanity that resulted.

Today's Challenge: Allow Christ's presence to transform your life, especially through the breaking of the bread in the Eucharist.

"Guide and Instruct"

by Joshua Bachman

Nov 22

An Ethiopian came to Jerusalem to worship. Philip heard him reading Isaiah the prophet, and he asked, "Do you understand what you are reading?" And he said, "How can I, unless someone guides me?" ~ Acts 8:27,30-31

God used Philip to guide the Ethiopian to the truth about God. Like the Ethiopian's lack of understanding about God, many in our society lack understanding about human life. A co-worker felt uneasy when she learned that some expectant mothers selectively abort based on gender when pregnant with multiple children. This conversation gave me an opportunity to help her understand that all abortions deny life to a human. "Always be prepared to make a defense to anyone who calls you to account for the hope that is in you, yet do it with gentleness and reverence."

Today's Challenge: Pray for those who are indifferent to the loss of human life through abortion, that they may seek truth.

Nov 23

"Heroic not Casual"
by Steve Castle

Jesus said to them, "Amen, amen, I say to you, unless you eat the flesh of the Son of Man and drink His blood, you do not have life within you." ~ Jn 6:53

Jesus made a series of radical statements to thousands of Jews following Him at the expense of watching them walk away thinking he was crazy. In many ways the issue of mandated abortion coverage in our health care system is eerily similar. To talk openly against it immediately divides and polarizes the audience. Jesus was exhorting the crowd to see the most profound heroic truth - something that stretched them - the Eucharist. Likewise, we must consider a profound truth that is stretching us to be heroic - defending the unborn.

Today's Challenge: Pray for our leaders and to make a commitment to always defend life.

"Value of Life"
by Dr. Kevin Vost

Nov 24

So, whatever you wish that men would do to you, do so to them; for this is the law and the prophets. ~ Mt 7:12

Many in our modern world deny the infinite value of every human life, from conception until natural death. The mother's womb, for example, crafted to nourish and nurture new human life, has now become the most dangerous location on earth. In a culture of death, they have been acculturated to perceive abortion as a morally neutral, medical decision. The innocent lives who have suffered the human sacrifice of choice get to make no choices of their own. Let us be sure then to hate and fight against the sin of abortion, while we love and fight for those who have been seduced by the wickedness and snares of the culture of death.

Today's Challenge: Educate those around you that abortion is the leading cause of death in the world.

Nov 25

"All In"
by Steve Castle

You shall love the Lord, your God, with all your heart, with all your soul, and with all your mind. ~ Mt 22:37

Jesus explains that all the prophets and all the law can be summed up in loving God and neighbor. It is the definition of "all in." I experienced an "all in" moment on a training run. I got into trouble on a desolate stretch of trail. After getting sick and running out of water I realized that I was beginning to show signs of heat exhaustion. I quietly recalled how the prophet Elijah curled up under the broom tree and prayed for death. I came around a bend and saw a lone shade tree, my broom tree. I laid under it and resigned to the good life God had given me. If ever I was "all in" I knew it was then. It was just me and God. I had no fear. My story ends well with a good Samaritan happening upon me. I knew what it was to be "all in" and the peace that awaits each of us.

Today's Challenge: Are you "all in"? All In Christ for Pro-Life!

"Stop the Train!"
by Dr. Patrick Castle

Nov 26

David regretted having numbered the people, and said to the Lord, I have sinned grievously in what I have done.
~ 2 Sm 24:10

David was counting because he lost faith that God provided enough for the war. Outside an abortion facility, an army of one person is enough to show the love of Christ to a mother and father, so they can stop the abortion. 9 million lives were lost in the Nazi concentration camps, and 42 million lives were lost to abortion in the year 2019 alone. While touring Dachau Concentration Camp, I heard a story that German church services would sing louder to drown out the cries of people on the trains going to the concentration camps. Our culture is doing exactly that today, singing over the reality of abortion. We will not sing over the cries of abortion-vulnerable mothers and fathers going to abortion facilities. We will help them stop those trains!

Today's Challenge: Let your Pro-Life F.A.C.E. shine! Faith, Action, Courts, Education.

Nov 27

"From the Cross"
by Deacon Sam Lee

Jesus rebuked Peter and said, "Get behind Me, satan. You are thinking not as God does, but as human beings do.
~ Mk 8:33

St. John Paul II reminds us, "we too find ourselves in the midst of a dramatic conflict between the culture of death and the culture of life. But the glory of the cross is not overcome by this darkness; rather, it shines forth ever more radiantly and brightly, and is revealed as the center, meaning, and goal of all history and of every human life." We must embrace the crosses in our life, which requires dying to self in service to others. We must always thank God for our crosses. They are a gift and opportunity to grow in holiness and enrich our relationship with Him.

Today's Challenge: View our crosses as gifts in the service of life.

"Love is Action"
by Fr. Jonathan St. Andre

Nov 28

Children, let us love not in word or speech but in deed and truth. ~ 1 Jn 3:18

There is a saying that "love has legs." In other words, the very essence of love is action. Philip not only told Nathaniel about Jesus, but he invited him and brought him to see Jesus. This is a perennial challenge for us as Christians in Pro-Life ministry. Is there enough evidence in our actions to convict us as followers of Jesus who are seeking to protect and promote life? We must use our gifts, like Philip did.

Today's Challenge: Do one action of deed and truth that reflects your deep conviction of the value of human life. Pray at an abortion facility, thank a Pro-Life doctor, donate clothes to a shelter, etc.

Nov 29

"When Evil Returns"
by Dr. Rich Reich

And they pleaded with Him, 'Send us into the swine. Let us enter them.' ~ Mk 5:12

Jesus cast out demons from the Gerasene demoniac. When the demons left the man's body, they did not disappear, but lingered about and occupied a nearby herd of swine. Jesus taught that an exorcised demon returns to its home "bringing back seven other spirits more wicked than itself." This serves as a warning to us. Do not become complacent. Remain alert, for evil will return with vengeance. Those who do God's will are not protected from evil attacks. Wear the belt of truth, the breastplate of righteousness, sandals of peace, the shield of faith, the helmet of salvation, and the sword of the Spirit. Stand firm in God and continue to pray for your brothers and sisters in Christ as we fight against the demon of abortion.

Today's Challenge: Protect yourself against evil by wearing the full armor of God.

"Prepare The Way"
by Bishop Joseph Coffey

Nov 30

Behold, I am sending My messengers ahead of you, he will prepare your way before you. ~ Lk 7:27

When I was in the seminary, a group of us would pray the Rosary every Friday afternoon across the street at a hospital that performed abortions. Sometimes people would curse at us, laugh at us, mock us. One day a man screamed at us, "Get a job!" How ironic yelling that to a bunch of men studying to be priests. I remember thinking, "Well, I guess this is my job, to pray for conversion, to publicly witness against the injustice of abortion, to stand up for the sanctity of all human life, especially the unborn child." John the Baptist had the job of preparing the way of the Lord. His stand for truth cost him his head. We may be mocked. We may be abused. We may someday even have to die for our faith. May God give us the courage and the grace to do His will no matter what the cost.

Today's Challenge: Prepare to be mocked for your faith, truth will set us free.

Dec 1

"Arms Wide Open"
by Lisa Skowron

Come to Me, all you who are weary and burdened, and I will give you rest. Take My yoke upon you and learn from Me, for I am gentle and humble in heart, and you will find rest for your souls. ~ Mt 11:28-29

I picture Jesus standing with arms wide open, ready to comfort me. As a child, it was the picture hanging on the wall in my church. But as I grew up, that childhood picture began to fade. I could no longer think of standing in Jesus' presence. Shame and guilt kept my eyes turned away from God because I had aborted my son Jonathan. I could not imagine that God would ever forgive me for that. I worked extremely hard over the years to keep those painful memories pushed down deep, and I felt completely separated from God. But when I broke my silence, all I received was His grace and compassion. I began to cherish time with God, running with Him instead of from Him. In Christ, my soul finally found rest.

Today's Challenge: A mission field has been created by abortion, and it exists all around us. Pray for post-abortion recovery programs.

"Speak Up"
by Dr. Patrick Castle

Dec 2

I speak this in the world so that they may share My joy completely. ~ Jn 17:13

Many people came together to search six times for even one more survivor amongst the devastation from the Joplin tornado. Most people speak up whenever they see something unsafe that could cost even one life. Why don't most people speak up about the horror of thousands of unborn children being aborted daily? Sin damages, intertwines and paralyzes. However, if we speak up, Christ can untangle and heal us. Speaking up also warns others about the lies of abortion, it builds guardrails to prevent others from going over the abortion cliff.

Today's Challenge: Speak up and cry out to build guardrails that protect unborn children and their families.

Dec 3

"Guideposts"
by Steve Castle

In those days He departed to the mountain to pray, and He spent the night in prayer to God. ~ Lk 6:12

Hope, patience, and prayer are beacons of faith laid before us, our guideposts. Jesus sets the example for us in prayer. He turned to the Father and spent the night with Him in prayer just prior to choosing the twelve apostles. It is important to note that Jesus also prayed at His baptism, before questioning the apostles about His identity, at His transfiguration, before teaching the apostles to pray, and His last words on the cross was a prayer. As Paul exhorts us in Ephesians, "pray at all times in the Spirit."

Today's Challenge: As we battle to end abortion, use the faith guideposts: hope, patience, and prayer.

"Triumph of The Cross"
by Stephanie Kemp

Dec 4

The Son of Man must be lifted up as Moses lifted up the serpent in the desert, so that everyone who believes in Him may have eternal life. ~ Jn 3:14-15

St. John Damascene wrote, "The cross is God's instrument to lift up those who have fallen, to support those who are still on their feet fighting. It is a crutch for the crippled and a guide for the wayward." If we embrace the cross with love, it can be a source of life and joy. In addition to praying at home or in church, we need to remember that Jesus went to the people, where He was most needed. We will never know how many lives have been saved as a result of prayer at abortion facilities, especially when Jesus is included there in the Eucharist.

Today's Challenge: Joyfully embrace the cross of Pro-Life ministry and help others carry theirs with courage and humility, no matter the cost.

Dec 5

"Pro-Life Surge"
by Dr. Patrick Castle

But you, go and proclaim the Kingdom of God. ~ Lk 9:60

This verse inspires us to surge out into the world, All In Christ for Pro-Life! With our country literally deadlocked on abortion, the LIFE Runners A-Cross America Relay provides a 40-day strategic surge for saving the unborn. We cannot protect the unborn if we stay hunkered down in ministries, which is like not going out from a military Forward Operating Base (FOB) in a hazardous area. LIFE Runners answer Christ's command to go out into the streets proclaiming, witnessing and serving. We need to leave the FOB in order to help untangle hearts and minds, aligning them with a culture of life.

Today's Challenge: Surge out of your FOB to help catalyze a culture of life. Bring a friend or a convoy to an abortion facility for life-saving prayer and advocacy.

"Rejoice!"

by Nellie Edwards

Dec 6

When they came out of the water, the Spirit of the Lord snatched Philip away, and the eunuch saw him no more, but continued on his way rejoicing. ~ Act 8:39

God's word reminds us that the joy of the Lord is my strength! The eunuch, who was stripped of his masculinity, is immersed in the living water of baptism and finds total fulfillment in Christ. Though Philip is suddenly snatched from him, the eunuch still rejoices because he is a new creation and has true joy. We lost a full-term baby without any indication of anything wrong, she was snatched away from us. I was able to cradle her for some time, and I thought my heart would explode from sorrow. By the grace of God, we relied on His word and thanked Him for His holy will, however painful. God's grace soon gave us peace and joy. In the midst of life's trials, let's have joy in knowing what awaits us, rejoice!

Today's Challenge: Help abortion-vulnerable parents feel joy by our love and support, so they see life as a true gift from God.

Dec 7

"Face of God"
by Nellie Edwards

Now the Earth was a formless void. There was darkness over the deep, and a divine wind sweeping over the waters. ~ Gen 1:2

I cannot help but relate the creation of the world to our own creation - beginning as formless matter. I picture how He intricately knitted us together in our mother's womb. It seems that God's creation of a human person was an even more daunting task than creating water, land, and air. We are His masterpiece and crowning glory of all creation! We can be inspired by majestic mountains, rainbows, and oceans - but all we must do is look at one another to see the face of God. Let us renew our prayers, penances, and political efforts to protect those whom He has lovingly made.

Today's Challenge: Tell abortion workers that you care about them. They are wounded souls who need the love and life of Christ.

"Moral Courage"
by Joe Hourigan

Dec 8

God formed man out of dust of the ground and blew into his nostrils the breath of life, and so man became a living being. ~ **Gen 2:7**

God breathed life into us and counts every conceived baby as one of His children. Knowing that abortion attacks the sanctity of life, I was led to prayerfully stand up for God's littlest ones in front of Planned Parenthood. God is giving those who are seeking to do His will, the moral courage to stand up and be a voice for those without one. "Few souls understand what God would accomplish in them if they were to abandon themselves unreservedly to Him and if they were to allow His grace to mold them accordingly." I pray for the grace to have courage to continue spreading the message of life-giving love, and to let God do whatever He chooses with my efforts for the least of these.

Today's Challenge: Consider praying every week outside your local abortion facility until the killing of innocent children ends.

Dec 9

"Get Service"
by Dr. Patrick Castle

Wisdom breathes life into her children and admonishes those who seek her. He who loves her loves life; those who seek her will be embraced by the Lord. ~ Sir 4:11-12

I recently saw a wisdom-filled short video called "Get Service." The video shows a man getting upset with the shortcomings of others until someone gives him special glasses to see everyone's crosses. This changed his perspective and drew him closer to Jesus' message to love our enemies. As our enemies force us to wait - too slow in line, driving under the speed limit - let's use this time to wait upon the Lord. Let's go the extra mile in our efforts for Pro-Life!

Today's Challenge: Imagine if we could see the crosses of those walking into the abortion facilities. Let's "Get Service" and bless them by offering them help.

"Sensationally Tangled"
by Dr. Patrick Castle

Dec 10

Is it lawful to do good on the sabbath rather than to do evil, to save life rather than to destroy it? But they remained silent. ~ Mk 3:4

With astronomical numbers of pregnancies ending in abortion, the death and damage has caused a sensationally tangled mess that has silenced many friends, families and professionals from sharing the truth. After sharing a video about a twin surviving an abortion, I received a message from a pro-choice therapist friend who said, "sensational videos can be very damaging." Abortion is by definition sensational, much like a horrific mass murder trial or the unthinkable Nazi extermination camps. Life is indeed complex, but all babies have the right to live, in all situations. The simple truth is that abortion kills a baby and damages a family, but Christ restores. The body of Christ has the power in Jesus' name to untangle this evil abortion mess and weave a culture of life.

Today's Challenge: Courageously speak the simple truth to prevent the death and damage of abortion.

Dec 11

"Take a Stand"
by Pastor Don Bird

He had cured many and, as a result, those who had diseases were pressing upon Him to touch Him. And whenever unclean spirits saw Him they would fall down before Him and shout, "You are the Son of God." ~ Mk 3:10-11

God wants to have a personal relationship with us, and He has come to confront satan and strip him of his power. Jesus tells us that evil no longer has reign in our lives. He demonstrates this not only in His power to heal and cast out demons, but in His desire to reclaim His territory! As His disciples, we promise to allow Him to work through us to reclaim the dark corners of our world – the street corners where drugs are sold, the bridges where the homeless sleep, and the abortion facilities where children are dying. We serve a God who has already claimed those places as His.

Today's Challenge: In what ways is God calling you to partner with Him to reclaim the dark areas in the world?

"Keep the Faith"
by Dr. Rich Reich

Dec 12

Once I said in my anguish, 'I am shut out from Your sight,' Yet You heard my plea, when I cried out to You. ~ Ps 31:22

Sometimes when we are suffering, it overwhelms our spirit, and we lose all hope in Christ. We feel that we are "shut out from His sight" and that we are all alone. We need to remember that we are never alone in our suffering. Our Lord even hears the cry of the suffering unborn and touches our hearts to defend them. When you feel that everything seems to be happening to you - poor health, unemployment, troubled marriage, etc. - keep the faith; for the Lord knows our suffering and "protects the loyal."

Today's Challenge: St. John Bosco taught us that "visits to the Blessed Sacrament are powerful and indispensable means of overcoming the attacks of the devil. Make frequent visits to Jesus in the Blessed Sacrament and the devil will be powerless against you." Prioritize spending time with Him daily.

Dec 13

"Identity"
by Dr. Rich Reich

Paul, a slave of God and apostle of Jesus Christ. ~ Tit 1:1

Outside of an abortion facility, we prayed for all those who were troubled by their pregnancy to receive grace to trust in God's will. We prayed that people might realize that abortion is not about children who "might" come into the world, but is about children who are already in the world, living and growing in the womb, and are scheduled to be killed. We prayed that people would realize the childrens' identity - they are not the property of their parents, nor of the government, but truly belong to God.

Today's Challenge: How do you as a Christian identify yourself? If you are Pro-Life, is it apparent in your actions?

"Run to Win"
by Dr. Allen Unruh

Dec 14

Do you not know that in a race all the runners run, but only one gets the prize? Run in such a way as to get the prize. ~ 1 Cor 9:24

The apostle Paul compared life to a race. Are you determined to endure to the end - to cross the finish line of life - and to never quit? We must take charge of our lives. By their fruits you shall know them. And what are the fruits of the Spirit? "They are love, joy, peace, longsuffering, kindness, goodness, faithfulness, gentleness, self-control." Can one person make a difference? Yes, God can use just one person to change the world if one has faith, even as small as a mustard seed. Always remind yourself that you can do all things through Christ who strengthens you.

Today's Challenge: Everything you think, say and do makes a difference in the lives of the people you meet and mentor. Decide now to make your mark, for Pro-Life!

Dec 15

"Faith and Humility"
by Dr. Rich Reich

The centurion said in reply, 'Lord, I am not worthy to have You enter under my roof; only say the word and my servant will be healed.' ~ Mt 8:8

The centurion demonstrates tremendous faith and humility. Even Jesus was amazed, "Amen, I say to you, in no one have I found such faith." The centurion, a military officer who commanded a hundred men, was also very humble in acknowledging in front of his men that he was "not worthy to have Jesus enter under his roof." Many post-abortion men and women feel that they are unworthy of God's forgiveness and healing. Jesus reminds us that "those who are well have no need of a physician. I have not come to call the righteous, but sinners to repentance."

Today's Challenge: Reach out to post-abortion loved ones with healing resources like Project Rachel and Rachel's Vineyard.

"Harvest Time"
by Dr. Patrick Castle

Dec 16

For we are God's co-workers; you are God's building.
~ 1 Cor 3:9

Although God could certainly plant and harvest without our help, He invites us to be part of His mighty work. Contemplating this helps bring the humility needed for God to help us tear down the world walls that we allow to slowly form around us. In humility, let us cry out for God's mercy and grace. "Do not conform any longer to the pattern of this world, then you will be able to test and approve what God's will is - His good, pleasing, and perfect will." Once we let those world walls crumble in God's hands, the healing begins, love grows, and God can welcome us as His co-workers.

Today's Challenge: Ask God what He would like you to do today for His Pro-Life work.

Dec 17

"Confidence in Jesus"
by Dr. Rich Reich

You will not abandon my soul to the nether world.
~ Ps 16:10

We can face death with confidence knowing that it is not the end. Our confidence in Christ should aspire to be as strong as St. Paul's, who said, "For to me life is Christ and death is gain." He looked forward to death with keen anticipation saying, "I long to depart this life and be with Christ, for that is far better." Have confidence that Jesus will not abandon our soul to the nether world. Death is merely the portal of eternal life.

Today's Challenge: Generously support life from concepttion to eternity.

"Stop Running Wild"
by Dr. Patrick Castle

Dec 18

Who do the crowds say that I am? ~ Lk 9:18

God is with us every moment and every season. When I sense God, I refer to that as a "God sighting." With respect to a "God sighting" there are no false positives, only false negatives. It is also important to listen for the presence of the Spirit. God is in the details. We need to slow down and consider those details. God, help me live in an awareness of your constant presence. We all need to do exactly that each day to prevent the golden calves from running wild in our life.

Today's Challenge: Courageously share Pro-Life truth to create social tension for exposing abortion's unjust peace, rebuilding a culture of life and setting the unborn free!

Dec 19

"Burn Brightly"
by Dr. Patrick Castle

I know your works, your labor, and your endurance, yet I hold this against you, you have lost the love you had at first. ~ Rev 2:2,4

How do we allow our love, our witness, and our passion to burn brightly without feeling worn down, tired, and exhausted after a while? "It is useless for you to work so hard from early morning until late at night, for God gives rest to his loved ones. To burn brightly without burning out, we stay connected to God. As each part does its own special work, it helps the other parts grow, so that the whole body is healthy and growing and full of love." We don't have to do everything on our own! May we know our need for God and our need for each other. God created us to stay connected to Him and to one another.

Today's Challenge: Get involved in worship, small groups, or a Bible study. It is so vital and important to live life abundantly, as God intends.

"Brother's Keeper"
by Dr. Rich Reich

Dec 20

Stop judging and you will not be judged. Stop condemning and you will not be condemned. Forgive and you will be forgiven. ~ Lk 6:37

A chief value of our culture today is tolerance; however, tolerance is not a Christian virtue. The Lord commands us not to judge or condemn others, but this does not mean to ignore sin and do nothing. Whether we want to admit it or not, we are our brother's keeper. We are called to warn, intercede for, teach, prophesy to, and serve sinners. We are ministers of reconciliation. We have a responsibility to protect others from sin, especially the sin of abortion. Do not be tolerant of abortion. Protect families from abortion by showing them God's love.

Today's Challenge: In a culture of tolerance, we cannot afford to be tolerant of abortion. Hate the sin of abortion, but love those affected by the sin.

Dec 21

"What do you want?"
by Bernadette Costello

What do you want Me to do for you? ~ **Mk 10:51**

How generous Jesus is to ask us such a question. Most of us can recall times that we have begged God for certain things in prayer instead of trusting the outcome that He wills for us. Especially when unexpected circumstances occur, such as an unplanned pregnancy, unhealthy child, or loss of a loved one. We can always count on God to provide us with an abundance more than we need. His burden is light, and only in Him will we find rest. He is always stretching His arms out to embrace us. Raise your hands high and praise Him at all times. He is always listening, and He will help you carry your burden. The most difficult times in life are, in time, the most cherished.

Today's Challenge: Spend time in the physical presence of Jesus in the monstrance at adoration. He tirelessly awaits you, go to Him.

"Live for Him"
by Bernadette Costello

Dec 22

We have given up everything and followed You.
~ Mk 10:28

Thank God every day that you awake. Thank Him for His creation of the world and all the people in it. He gave His very life for each one of us, and He continues to share His passion with us thousands of times daily all over the world in each Mass that is celebrated. Choose to follow Him now in order to live eternal life with Him later. Is your most prized possession worth more to you than eternal life? Give it away! Live your life for Him. Feed and clothe the poor, visit the sick and imprisoned, and be the face of God at abortion facilities to help our lost brothers and sisters find their way back to Christ.

Today's Challenge: Spend time speaking to God about everything in your life. Thank Him for all that He has given you, which is everything.

Dec 23

"Conception to natural death"
by Dr. Patrick Castle

Teacher, we want You to do for us whatever we ask of You. ~ Mk 10:35

Capital punishment was needed in the Old and New Testaments because government was not able to control super criminals. Capital punishment is not necessary today with our super prisons. Do you think it is easier to die by lethal injection or be in prison for life? Some say that certain criminals deserve to die. Spiritually speaking, we all deserve to die, but are saved by accepting the gift of Christ's cross. Can you imagine being the innocent person who endured trial, appeals, and execution? This is what Christ went through for us. Regardless of our views on capital punishment, we are called by Christ to love and forgive even the worst criminals.

Today's Challenge: Make use of the whole armor of God to withstand evil. Battle for life from conception to natural death without any compromise.

"Hope-Filled Crisis"
by Dr. Patrick Castle

Dec 24

He has raised up for us a mighty Savior, born of the house of His servant David. ~ Lk 1:69

Mary's hope-filled crisis pregnancy pierced the darkness forever when the Christ child was born into the world. We open our arms to hold baby Jesus knowing that our mighty Savior will open His arms on the cross to hold us for eternity. Christ chose to become poor for our sake, yet our world chooses to abort millions of children because they are poor. God meets us in our poverty. May we empty ourselves at His feet, so we can be fed with His Body!

Today's Challenge: Pause and reflect in front of a crucifix - oh, how He loves us.

Dec 25

"Merry Christmas"
by Fr. Daren Zehnle

She wrapped Him in swaddling clothes and laid Him in a manger, because there was no room for them in the inn.
~ Lk 2:7

If we were present in that stable, we likely would have swept the straw into nice piles or perhaps even constructed a makeshift bed for Mary, all with the aim of making things better suited for Jesus. Yet what we see in His birth is that the Lord comes precisely into the messiness of our lives without seeming to worry about how untidy our lives may be; what is necessary is that He is welcomed. As LIFE Runners we help women who feel burdened, trapped, and forced into abortion to recognize that Jesus wishes to come into the messiness of their lives as well, asking only that He be welcomed.

Today's Challenge: Remember that the Christ child was born into the messiness of our human world. Surrender yourself to God in your own messy life.

"Hope in the Lord"

by Bernadette Costello

Dec 26

I wait for the Lord, my soul waits, and in His word I hope.
~ Ps 130:5

God whispers hope, truth, and life. Satan whispers shame, fear, and death. He says that God will abandon us and that we should be afraid. Satan is a liar. He tries to steal our hope, joy, and life. Countless people are spiritually wounded by our dark secular world and are in desperate need of healing.

Today's Challenge: There is a limitless outpouring of mercy for all contrite souls. Share God's news of hope and healing with post-abortion parents who are suffering.

Dec 27

"Our Actions Matter"
by Bernadette Costello

Whoever then relaxes one of the least of these commandments and teaches men so, shall be called least in the kingdom of Heaven. ~ Mt 5:19

We cannot ignore God's commandments. He does not suggest or ask us to follow His laws but commands us. Furthermore, He commands us to teach and encourage others to follow Him and His commandments. He knows our human weaknesses and knows that we need an outpouring of His graces to achieve something so great. We must live in unceasing prayer so that every action with another is an interaction with Christ. We cannot earn our way into Heaven, but we can count on God's words - he who follows the commandments and teaches them shall be called great in the kingdom of Heaven.

Today's Challenge: Live so that your actions speak boldly that you are All In Christ for Pro-Life!

"Prayer"
by Dianne Overmann

Dec 28

Jesus departed to the mountain to pray, and He spent the night in prayer to God. ~ Lk 6:12

In a day-to-day conversation, I admit to using "I will pray for you" to respond to another's problem. I have noticed that others will stop and say, "Let's pray together." Is there not a big difference? My niece was beginning a teaching job in a new school. Like most, she was nervous the first day. Another teacher whispered into her ear a prayer for God's peace and guidance. Is that not the loving touch of God?

Today's Challenge: Give two minutes a day in your imagination to embrace a woman making a life decision for her child. Pray with her.

Dec 29

"Spell Life"
by Dianne Overmann

Do not be anxious about anything, but in everything, by prayer and petition with thanksgiving present your request to God. ~ Phil 4:6

I know that the witness of my life can touch others. Recently, a lady whispered to me that she was in a difficult situation, then asked me to spell "abortion clinic." I reminded her that she was talking about a human being. She told me she had been in an accident and didn't think she could raise the child. I promised her that I would pray that she would listen to God and choose Life. She agreed to pray and to talk to her husband. I did not expect God to show me the love not only for this child, but for this mother. I could feel God embrace her through me. Let's pray that we can courageously help others spell "Life."

Today's Challenge: Please take 5 minutes today to pray not just for the unborn, but for those mothers who are so afraid and anxious.

"Sabbath Walk"
by Dianne Overmann

Dec 30

You are not made for the Sabbath; the Sabbath is made for you. ~ Mk 2:27

I am reminded that God commands me to stop and harness the violence of busyness. Even when I dedicate my life to the service of others, the frantic over activity can cause suffering to others and to myself. The lack of rest and reflection can limit my ability to live in wonder and awe at the greatness of God. When I consecrate time to be still, my service to others is filled with grace and everyone is blessed. Sabbath is a way of remembering who I am, what I know, and helps me to taste the gifts of the Spirit and eternity. I need to take delight in my life and the fruits of the Spirit. I need to rid myself of the feeling of guilt in taking time to rest and to be with God. The Creator invites me to take seriously His Commandment to step back and take a Sabbath walk, to see the sacredness of life.

Today's Challenge: Take 5 minutes each day to be silent and hear the voice of God.

Dec 31

"Seeing Life is Believing Life"
by Dr. Kevin Vost

Have you come to believe because you have seen Me? Blessed are those who have not seen and have believed. ~ Jn 20:29

The Apostle Thomas, the world's most famous doubter, declared he would not believe that Christ was alive until he saw the nail marks in His hands, put his fingers into those nail marks, and put his hand into His side. Christ, of course, obliged him, but then blessed those who believed without seeing. There was a time I considered myself an unbeliever in Christ, and sympathetic to some pro-choice arguments. After two miscarriages, my wife was advised to have an amniocentesis. One glance at the screen of that high-quality ultrasound and I would never consider an unborn child a potential life again.

Today's Challenge: Encourage women showing up at abortion facilities to experience the power of ultrasound images to awaken them to the truth of the real human life within their womb.

Authors Index

Tess Allman	Aug 9
Pavel Arestov	Feb 3
John Audino	Oct 13
Joshua Bachman	Aug 8, Sep 13, Nov 22
Dale Bartscher	Mar 10
Sara Beaner	Jan 22, Apr 21
Rosemary Bernth	Feb 23
Fr. Vince Bertrand	Sep 25
Pastor Don Bird	Mar 30, Apr 12, 19, Jun 11, Jul 10, 29, Nov 5, Dec 11
Peggy Bowes	May 4, Jun 15
Beth Bubik	Mar 4
Pastor Ron Burtz	Oct 7
Scott Casmer	Jan 2, Apr 3, 15, 30, May 11, 20, Aug 22, 26
Angi Castle	Jan 31, Mar 26, Apr 26, Jun 2
Kathy Castle	Apr 5

Paige Castle	Nov 11
Dr. Patrick Castle	Jan 23, Feb 14, 15, 16, Mar 2, 25, Apr 11, 17, 28, May 19, 24, 27, 28, 29, Aug 28, Sep 19, Oct 26, 27, 30, Nov 4, 9, 16, 26, Dec 2, 5, 9, 10, 16, 18, 19, 23, 24
Steve Castle	Jan 1, Apr 6, Nov 13, 23, 25, Dec 3
Alice Chapman	Feb 8, Apr 20, Jun 9, 21, Jul 20, Aug 20, Sep 26
Dana Cody	Jan 9
Bishop Joseph Coffey	Sep 11, Nov 30
Whitney Compton	Aug 13, 25
Carol Cooper	Mar 22
Bernadette Costello	Jun 10, 14, 18, 27, 28, 30, Jul 2, 22, 27, Aug 2, 7, 11, 12, Dec 21, 22, 26, 27
Fr. James Dean	Jul 3, 17
Fr. Justin Dean	Nov 17
Fr. Andrew Dickinson	Jan 11, Feb 25

Dave Dinuzzo	Feb 17
TD Dorrell	Feb 2
Laurie Edwards	Oct 21
Nellie Edwards	Dec 6, 7
Grant Fenske	Mar 7
Kathy Forck	Jan 19, Apr 9, Jul 1
Pastor Rick Foreman	Apr 10, May 2, Jun 1, 29, Jul 26, Aug 10
Jenn Garza	Jan 27, Feb 12, Oct 9
Jeff Grabosky	Jan 14, 20, Apr 2, May 1, 15
Mary Grabosky	Mar 27, Apr 24, May 30, Jun 8
Bishop Robert Gruss	Mar 28
Ed Heigl	Apr 25, May 26, Jul 25, Sep 7, Nov 1
Kristina Hernandez	Nov 18
Mary Ellen Hoffman	Jun 20
Stephen Holinaty	Jul 13, Oct 5
Barb Honeycutt	Sep 28
Joe Hourigan	Mar 16, Dec 8

Abby Johnson	May 16
Valerie Johnson	Feb 19
Peter Kahama	May 8
Shane Kapler	Jan 28, Feb 6, 18, 22, 26, Mar 21, Jun 24, Aug 31, Sep 5, 10, 22, Oct 11, 14, 17, 19, 25
Stephanie Kemp	Jan 17, Mar 13, Dec 4
Amy Kosta	Jan 30, Feb 11, Mar 31, Apr 23, Jun 12, Jul 11, Aug 4
Matthew Laugeman	Mar 14, Jul 4, Oct 1
Teresa Laugeman	Nov 20
Deacon Sam Lee	Mar 20, Nov 27
Finau Leggett	Jun 4
Pastor Matthew Lim	Sep 15, Oct 15
Kathryn Lopez	Apr 8, Nov 8
Kevin Lowry	Nov 21
Jimmy Mack	Aug 1
Dr. Sebastian Mahfood	May 13
Jeanne Mancini	Jan 10

Brandon McAuliffe	Jul 12
Molly McDonald	Jan 18, Feb 13
Kevin McNicholas	Jan 25, Jun 25, Jul 15, 18, Aug 19, 21, Sep 1, 12, 16
Daria Monroe	Mar 5
Lauren Muzyka	Feb 9, Apr 16, Aug 14, Sep 23
Governor Kristi Noem	Oct 31
Karen Nolkemper	Apr 13
Jean Noon	Sep 17
Paul Nurse	Sep 21
Fr. Joseph Oganda	Aug 29, Nov 3
Fr. Michael Orsi	Feb 1
Dianne Overmann	Jan 12, Feb 29, May 5, 21, Jul 7, Sep 14, Dec 28, 29, 30
Dr. Cliff Ozmun	Nov 7
Bishop Thomas Paprocki	Mar 1, Oct 28
Allan Parker	Jan 15
Paula Parmelee	Apr 29, Jun 17, Jul 8
Karen Patnaude	Apr 1

Alton Pelowski	Jan 3, Feb 7
Jason Peters	Feb 10
Dr. Rich Reich	Jan 6, 8, 13, 16, 24, 26, 29 Feb 4, 5, 24, Mar 8, 15, 19 Apr 4, 18, 22, May 10, 14, 18, 25, 31 Jun 3, 6, 7, 13, 16, 19, 22, 23, 26 Jul 6, 9, 14, 19, 21, 24, 28, 30 Aug 3, 15, 16, 17, 18, 23, 24, 30 Sep 3, 6, 8, 20, 24, 27, 29, 30 Oct 2, 6, 12, 18, 20, 23, 24 Nov 6, 10, 19, 29 Dec 12, 13, 15, 17, 20
Greg Robeson	Jan 7
Bonnie Sabin	Feb 28, May 22, Jul 5
Mike Sanders	Sep 18, Oct 3
Ann Schaefbauer	Apr 7
Stephen Schmidt	May 3
Pastor Steve Selfridge	Jan 4
Lisa Skowron	May 6, 12, Aug 5, Dec 1
Becky Soske	Feb 20

Jack Spring	Nov 15
Fr. Jonathan St. Andre	Mar 3, Jun 5, Aug 6, Nov 28
Dr. John Sturm	Mar 11, Jul 31, Sep 9, Oct 16
Chris Talley	Jul 16
Scofield Thomas	Oct 4
Dr. Gregory Thompson	Nov 14
Janice Todd	Mar 12
Fr. Joseph Totton	Nov 2
Dr. Allen Unruh	Dec 14
Bridget VanMeans	Mar 23
Dr. Kevin Vost	Mar 17, Apr 27, May 7, 9, 17, Sep 2, Oct 8, 22, 29, Nov 24, Dec 31
Deacon Bob Waller	Apr 14
Tonchi Weaver	Jan 21
Justin Weiler	Feb 21
Paul Westendorf	Jan 5, Mar 6, 29, Aug 27
Doug Wollman	Nov 12
Stacey Wollman	Mar 24, Jul 23, Oct 10

| Doug Young | Feb 27, Mar 18 |
| Fr. Daren Zehnle | Mar 9, May 23, Sep 4, Dec 25 |

Made in the USA
Monee, IL
27 January 2021